Fern
Sandwik
Burgh
Kinedar
Inverealan
Forlair
Pitsligo

Duflus
Elgin
Boyn
Fores
Fochopir
St Nicholas
Keth
Rothes
Abirterdour
Balvany
Rothemay
Tellie
Strathbolgy
Ellon
Slans
Achindoun
Gartly
Dunudeir
Meldrum
Forbes

Drumin
Tulanygus
Manymusk
Fintray
Balhelvy

Benachie
Kintore
Abirdon
Abirnethy
Kilbarthan
Don
Lumfinan
Abirdene
Kincardin
Kilblene
Obyn
Maryculir
Cammor
Strathhtt
Drum

Invarald
Brae Mar
W. of Der
Mearni
Fordun
Kincardin

Inverqubarty
Mumros
Blair
Kincoldrum
Brechin
Arly
Forfar
Guthery
Inverbrvan
Lognuth
Meml
Dunkeld
Cupir
Dundee

Single Malt
SCOTCH

Single Malt
SCOTCH

Bill Milne
Roddy Martine

FRIEDMAN/FAIRFAX
PUBLISHERS

A FRIEDMAN/FAIRFAX BOOK

© 1997 by Michael Friedman Publishing Group, Inc.

Library of Congress Cataloging-in-Publication Data

Martine, Roderick.
      Single malt scotch / Roddy Martine.
         p.   cm.
      Includes index.
      ISBN 1-56799-440-7
       1.   Whiskey—Scotland.I. Title.
TP605.M27   1997
641.2'52'0941- -dc21   97-7238

Editor: Tony Burgess
Art Director: Jeff Batzli
Designer: Garrett Schuh
Production Manager: Karen Matsu Greenberg
Photography Editor: Chris Bain

Color separations by Colourscan Overseas Co Pte Ltd
Printed in England by Butler and Tanner Ltd.

1 3 5 7 9 10 8 6 4 2

For bulk purchases and special sales, please contact:
Friedman/Fairfax Publishers
Attention: Sales Department
15 West 26th Street
New York, New York 10010
212/685-6610   FAX 212/685-1307

Visit our website:
http://www.metrobooks.com

DEDICATIONS

To Sheena McDonald.

—R.M.

To everyone who has asked me "So how is your book doing?" Also
to my dear friends Christopher Bain and Campbell Evans, without
whose help and encouragement this book would never have gotten
off the ground.

—B.M.

ACKNOWLEDGMENTS

In the course of preparing this book, I had the very pleasurable duty of traveling about the whisky-producing regions of Scotland, absorbing the history and ambiance of a world steeped in ancient tradition. And, of course, tasting a great deal of wonderful whisky.

Throughout my travels I was made to feel very welcome wherever I went, but three establishments are worthy of special mention. The Clifton House, in Nairn, is unique, and should not be missed if at all possible. Proprietor and chef J. Gordon McIntyre has an extraordinary talent for hospitality, and he is an absolute wizard in the kitchen. I cannot begin to thank Alan Hill, Executive Director of Food and Beverage at the Gleneagles Hotel in Auchterarder, for all his help and hospitality, and I am similarly indebted to Mark Barker, Executive Chef at the St. Andrews Old Course Hotel. Both the Gleneagles and the St. Andrews are exquisite resorts, with courteous staff, beautiful grounds and rooms, and, for lovers of either golf or Scotch whisky, full shares of history and tradition.

—Bill Milne

The following individuals all offered invaluable help and advice in creating this book, and I extend to them my heartfelt thanks:

John Ashworth, James Bruxner, Peter Darbyshire, Andrew Dewar-Durie, James Espey, Campbell Evans, John Goodwin, Alan Hill, Brian Ivory, Peter Lederer, James McColl, Lord Macfarlane of Bearsden, Alastair S. McIntosh, Gordon and Margaret McIntosh, Gordon McIntyre, Hector MacLennan, Hugh Morrison, W. Brian Morrison, Jill Preston, David Smith, Peter Smith, James Thompson, Jim Thurle, James Wolfe Murray.

—Roddy Martine

CONTENTS

INTRODUCTION

In the Gaelic language, the tongue of the native Highland Scot, Scotch whisky is known as *uisgebeatha*, which means "the water of life." For generations, Scotch has been a companion of celebration and a solace during Scotland's long, dark winter months.

There are approximately eighty-six distilleries currently operating in Scotland, but nobody fully comprehends why each produces an identifiably unique single-malt product. All Scotch whisky is manufactured from barley and the pure water of the Scottish mountains, and the process remains virtually the same at each distillery, yet a Laphroaig from Islay is different from a Bowmore produced on the same island, and very far removed from a Glenlivet from Speyside or a Glengoyne from Dunbarton.

The secret of Scotland's single-malts lies in the Scottish landscape, the great rush of water as it moves from the bens to the glens, and into the tumbling rivers and silent lochs. It lies in the aging process, which takes place in oak casks previously containing sherry or bourbon. And it lies in the peat fires of the furnaces, in the shape of the copper pot stills, in the mineral deposits and the plant life through which the water flows on its way to the distillery. All of these things play a significant part in somehow, magically, creating a unique single-malt.

Single-malt Scotch has been imitated, but never matched. Others, notably the Japanese, have attempted to copy the chemistry. While the imitations are similar, and in some cases excellent, they have not been the same.

Single-malt and blended Scotch whiskies have begun to achieve record levels of popularity, not only in North America and the United Kingdom, but in Asia and Eastern Europe as well. There are currently more than one hundred regional single-malts of different ages, and more than 122 blended products from Scotland to tempt the palates of the discerning Scotch whisky drinker. Many are not yet widely available in North America, but devotees of the spirit can obtain them through such organizations as the Scotch Malt Whisky Society, with branches in Scotland and the United States, which buys selected single-malts from the distilleries and bottles them straight from the cask under its own label for its members.

Thankfully, the image of the typical Scotch drinker as a tweedy old gent with a ruddy complexion has largely disappeared. Scotch whisky in all its varieties is now seen as the drink for the contemporary man and woman, a drink that reflects confidence, success, and sophistication.

The mystery of Scotch keeps it from being common, and the passion and loyalty of its drinkers raises it to a level above the ordinary. It is truly a remarkable creation.

page 8: Sunlight filters onto the malting floor at the Balvenie Distillery. *page 9: The Cragganmore 12-year-old single malt.* **opposite:** *Bricks of rich dark peat on the Island of Islay.* **above:** *The sweeping, fertile fields of Speyside, known locally as "The Drowned Land."*

1

The History of **SCOTCH WHISKY**

The original Scots, a Celtic race, came across the North Channel of the Atlantic

Ocean from Ireland to settle the mainland of northern Britain. Between A.D. 500

and 843 they slowly integrated with the Picts and various other indigenous tribes.

By the mid-ninth century, Kenneth MacAlpine, heir to the throne of Dalriada (the

Gaelic name for the Kingdom of Scots) through his father's marriage to a Pictish

princess, was able to claim the Pictish throne and unite the two kingdoms, which

became known as Alba, and later Scotland.

page 12: The gleaming copper surface of a wash still, where the spirit is first distilled from the fermented wash. **page 13:** *Sleeping casks of uisge-beatha lie undisturbed for years.* **right:** *The Kinchie Burn provides the water for the Glenkinchie Distillery, in East Lothian.*

One result of unification was that Christianity came to replace the ancient Druid culture. Monasteries and churches were established, and it is to here that the beginning of the Scotch industry can be traced. The practice of distillation is said to have been introduced in Scotland by St. Columba and his followers, who brought Christianity to the Hebridean island of Iona in A.D. 563. These monks and friars came over from Ireland, where it is claimed that St. Patrick had introduced the practice of distillation more than one hundred years earlier.

Distillation had been practiced by the church from earliest times although, as was the case in mainland Europe, it was used largely to produce brandy from wine and mead from fermented honey. Once it was discovered that barley would ferment to produce ale, it was a natural progression to move on to distillation.

The production of whisky from malted barley most likely started around the eleventh or twelfth century, by which time both the Scots and the Irish had become rather skilled in distillation. The earliest written reference to it in Scotland, however, dates from 1494, when an entry in the Exchequer Rolls records the despatch to Lindores Abbey, in the Kingdom of Fife on the east coast, of "eight bolls of malt to Friar John Cor wherein to make aqua vitae."

Eight bolls is the equivalent of half a ton of malt, and would have been enough to produce approximately seventy gallons of aqua vitae. There would have been much merriment following its delivery to the Court of James IV, King of Scots.

It is this date, 1494, that the Scotch Whisky Association, the trade association for the Scotch whisky industry, seized upon in

opposite: *Ripening malt is left to lie on the malting floor at the Balvenie Distillery.* **above:** *This display at the Scotch Whisky Heritage Centre in Edinburgh depicts an early distillery in progress.*

1994 as an excuse to celebrate five hundred years of the Spirit of Scotland. So although people had been making single-malt whisky for a very long time before this, 1494 is now recognized as its official birthday.

But making single-malt whisky in 1494 was no easy matter. Simple survival was difficult enough. Long winters, followed by damp summers, made life tough in the rugged Highlands of Scotland. While some opted to earn a living among the glens and moors of the far north by lying in wait for the unsuspecting traveler, the lifeblood of most Highlanders came from the cattle trade with the Lowlands. Farming communities would cultivate produce for these cattle during the summer, and with what was left

over, they would manufacture uisgebeathas during the dark winter months. Seasonally the cattle would be driven south along the drove roads, simple tracks through the mountains, to the cattle sales, or trysts, at Crieff or Falkirk, near Stirling, and often further afield to Edinburgh and Glasgow. As part of their cargo, the cattle drovers would often carry kegs of uisgebeatha, always easy to sell to the Lowland buyers at these trysts.

Early equipment used for making whisky was, of course, fairly primitive. It was difficult to measure the strength, or proof, of the whisky; the earliest known method was to set fire to a measure and see how much was left. Another test was to add a touch of gunpowder; if the whisky exploded, it was undoubtedly over-proof, indeed potentially lethal. If, on the other hand, it burned smoothly, then it was fine to drink.

In 1675, Robert Boyle invented "Boyle's Bubble," an instrument to measure specific gravities of liquids, but a reliable hydrometer capable of accurately gauging proof was not introduced until as late as 1818.

It was not until the eighteenth century that uisgebeatha was recognized as the national drink of Scotland. Until then, ale was much more popular with the lower classes, especially in the

top: *The cask firing process bonds the interior wood together and releases the surface flavors of the wood.* **opposite:** *A tranquil landscape on the grounds of the world-famous Gleneagles Hotel, near Auchterarder in Perthshire. The Gleneagles Hotel is considered to be one of the finest holiday resorts in the world.*

A TRADITIONAL BURNS SUPPER

Robert Burns, Scotland's national bard, was born on a farm at Alloway in Ayrshire on January 25, 1759. His humble origins and his identification with the Scottish folk tradition, which he rescued, won him unfailing and enduring popularity.

After his early death at the age of thirty-seven, dinners were held throughout Scotland to perpetuate his memory. With the mass emigration of Scots to the New World in the following centuries, the tradition was carried overseas and has become as popular, if not more so, than the annual St. Andrew's Day celebrations, which commemorate Scotland's patron saint.

At a traditional Burns Supper, a piper leads guests into dinner and is rewarded with a dram of Scotch. The first course usually consists of Cock-a-leekie soup, made from a fowl boiled with leeks, or a similar rich broth. The main course is haggis, neeps (puréed turnips), and tatties (puréed potatoes), and is heralded by Burns' "Address to the Haggis," usually delivered by the host of the occasion, who carves the haggis at the head of the table. The pudding course is invariably Atholl Brose, made from Scotch, honey, and oats whipped up in thick cream. An alternative or addition to this is a variety of Scottish cheese, such as Cabok or Lanarkshire Blue. Although wine is invariably poured, a single malt whisky is served with each course.

After dinner, speeches are made, the most important being "The Immortal Memory," when a guest well-versed in the work of Burns pays tribute to the poet and discusses his great contribution to humanity. Robert Burns loved women, many of them, and so there is always a "Toast to the Lassies," followed by a "Reply from the Lassies." In years gone by, Burns Suppers were an all-male affair, but nowadays both men and women enjoy the celebration.

The evening closes with readings from a selection of Burns' better known works, such as "Tam O' Shanter" and "Holy Willy's Prayer," and songs such as "My Love is Like a Red Red Rose" and "Ae Fond Kiss" are sung.

opposite: *This reproduction of an early whisky still shows how the spirit was condensed by passing through a copper coil with cool water flowing over it.*

above: *Most of the whisky produced in Scotland goes for blending; only a small percentage is bottled and sold in the form of a single-malt.*

Lowlands, where the majority of Scotland's population lived. Although uisgebeatha was drunk socially and medicinally, it was invariably served up as a punch with fruit and sugar added, or as Atholl Brose, a mixture of malt, honey, and oatmeal.

But in 1725, eighteen years after the Act of Union joined Scotland and England under one government, this new British government, in complete disregard of the terms of the Act of Union, imposed a tax on Scottish malt that forced brewers to raise their prices. Rioting immediately broke out in the streets of Edinburgh and Glasgow, where the house of the local member of Parliament was attacked. The protests, however, made little difference, and the tax remained in place.

Ale became increasingly more expensive, and the Lowland distilleries tried to keep their costs down by using unmalted barley,

above: *Flowers and greenery abound in the rich, verdant pastureland of the Scottish Highlands.* opposite: *A golden glass of Knockando single-malt specially drawn and bottled for Gordon McIntyre, proprietor of Clifton House, in 1960.*

but failed in making a palatable drink. The canny Scot soon realized that the only way to avoid paying the hated tax was to distill malt whisky illicitly.

Within a few decades, there were illegal stills operating all over the country, and the drinking habits of the Scots had changed. Ale was no longer considered the national drink of the Scots. Uisgebeatha had taken its place.

From 1784 onward, the British government continued to impose ever more punitive taxation against Scottish whisky distillers, and even those determined to stay within the law began to think again. Whereas the Lowlands were largely accessible to the police, many parts of the Highlands remained inaccessible to them. Illicit distilling became a cottage industry practiced on virtually every farm and small tenant share to supplement income. Without the money they earned from selling homemade uisgebeatha, most Highland tenant farmers over this period would have been unable to pay their rents.

Illicit stills varied enormously in shape and size. A simple version could be made from a cauldron with a cover and spout attached to a coil or spiral of copper tubing, most probably enclosed in a barrel through which flowed fresh water from a nearby burn. The fresh water was essential, for as it passed through the barrel, it

above: An exhibit at the Scotch Whisky Heritage Centre in Edinburgh.   **opposite:** *Packaged grain sits waiting at the Glengoyne Distillery, near Dunbarton.*

would cool and condense the hot spirit that entered the upper coil as a vapor.

Illicit stills needed to be easily portable. Often they were hidden close to a burn or running water, but sometimes in the most unlikely places, such as the vaults below the Free Tron Kirk, an important church in Edinburgh's High Street.

It was only a matter of time before the government realized that it would never win this ongoing battle, so a commission was set up to investigate the problem. In 1823, Parliament passed an act meant to put an end once and for all to illicit distilling. A registration fee about equal, in today's terms, to fifteen dollars was introduced on all stills of forty gallons or upwards, and distilleries were obliged to pay a duty on each gallon of spirits distilled. The fee and the duty combined were a good deal cheaper than the previous taxes on malt had been.

Although there was initial resistance, especially in the more remote corners of the far northeast of the country, within two years the quantity of uisgebeatha being declared for tax had risen from two million to six million gallons per annum. The long-term consequence of this act, therefore, was to transform a crofter's illegal pastime into a booming Scottish industry that, by the end of the nineteenth century, was making a significant and ever-increasing contribution toward the British economy.

All classes of society were partaking of Scotch whisky. Two things happened in the early nineteenth century that ensured the reputation of single malt whisky as a fashionable drink. Although uisgebeatha was widely drunk throughout the rural areas of Scotland, the landed gentry continued to stock port, claret, and brandy, all easily obtained from France, in the cellars of their great houses, as these drinks were still considered more sophisticated. All this was to change dramatically with the advent of the Napoleonic Wars at the turn of the nineteenth century. At the height of the hostilities with France, for example, the City Council of Edinburgh took a vote to ban the import of French claret "in order to bring the French Nation to its knees."

SCOTCH AT THE DINNER TABLE

Single malt Scotch whiskies have long been appreciated as the perfect after-dinner drink or nightcap, an ideal alternative to brandy, Cointreau, or other liqueurs. Likewise, it is quite common for Scotch whisky to be taken as an aperitif, though in this case a blended whisky, possibly in a cocktail, is more appropriate than a single-malt, whose relatively intense flavor should not be allowed to dull the palate before one is seated at the dinner table.

Scotch whisky is far less often appreciated as an accompaniment to food, and yet it really should not be overlooked as a delightful and intriguing alternative to wine. Clearly, the company must exercise a certain degree of moderation, as it is by no means difficult, over the course of a long, multicourse dinner, to become excessively intoxicated. But if consumption is kept to a reasonable level, and if care is taken in matching specific dishes with appropriate whiskies, then a sumptuous dinner party may also be an opportunity for friends to embark together upon a magical tour of Scotland, using single-malts as their guide. A light Glenkinchie or Glengoyne, for example, makes a fine companion for a starter dish. A nicely balanced Auchentoshan, or almost any Speyside malt, goes well with meat and game, while a vegetarian main course will go very nicely with a warm and malty product of the Eastern Highlands such as Fettercairn or Edradour. A Glenmorangie, Royal Lochnagar, or Cardhu complements a rich dessert delightfully, and an assertive Island malt such as Talisker or Lagavulin is a superb companion for a plate of cheese.

While it may strike some as a radical idea to serve Scotch whisky with food, one should never be too quick to rule out any of the myriad ways in which uisgebeatha may be enjoyed.

above: *Scotland's landscape is one of rich contrasts and wide open spaces ruled by the stag and the golden eagle.*

Whisky's reputation improved again in 1822, when King George IV visited Scotland and partook of Glenlivet. Thereafter to take a dram of uisgebeatha was seen among young men as a symbol of maturity and manhood.

As uisgebeatha solidified its place as the drink of the Scots, a number of social rituals became associated with it. In the Highlands of Scotland, a newborn baby might be welcomed into the world with a drop of Scotch on the tongue (which had much the same effect as a smack on the backside). Uisgebeatha was drunk at wedding receptions and at wakes, following funerals. When a piper was on hand to lead guests into dinner, his reward would be a dram.

Sales took off with the introduction of blended Scotch in the 1850s. By the end of the century brand names such as James Buchanan's Black and White, Peter Mackie's White Horse and Alexander Walker's Johnnie Walker had become famous. Between 1880 and 1925, Scotch whisky barons such as John and Tommy

opposite: *A bottle of Old Parr Superior sits amid a display of its components.* **above:** *Casks are stacked up at the Macallan Cooperage ready to be filled with the "water of life."*

opposite: *Casks of the Dalmore from 1969 await discovery.*   above left: *Pewter measuring jugs, parts of the stillman's toolkit.*

above right: *The famous Glenmorangie stencil, which identifies every cask.*

Dewar and John Haig founded empires that in turn were bought out to create even greater empires, notably the Distillers Company Ltd., now the giant United Distillers PLC, producer of ten single malt and twenty-two blended whiskies.

The popularity of single malt whisky moved beyond the borders of Scotland as the Scots themselves emigrated to new homes, notably the United States and Canada. Despite the fact that settlers in both these countries had already built their own grain distilleries, Scotch from Scotland proved immensely popular, to the extent that many U.S. distilleries were driven out of business. In 1891, a "Statement of Distillers" in the United States showed a total of 779 operational grain distillers, the largest number in North Carolina, followed by Kentucky. In 1903, the number had fallen to 613 and in 1914, to 434. By 1919, there were only thirty-four remaining, and then came thirteen years of Prohibition.

The advent of Prohibition in the United States in January 1920 had an inevitable impact upon export sales, and when Prohibition ended in 1933, a marketing initiative to restore Scotch to its pre-Prohibition popularity was launched. As it happened, the reputation of Scotch had survived remarkably well. Colm Brohan, in his book *The Glasgow Story*, published in 1952, writes that during the Prohibition period, American theater audiences were apt to laugh and cheer at any mention of the city of Glasgow on the screen. "They knew Glasgow as a city which produced whisky they could drink with confidence that their stomach lining would remain more or less where it was before."

The twentieth century witnessed several ups and downs in the industry. During the two world wars, grain was diverted to feed people in preference to making Scotch whisky for them to drink. During the depression of the 1930s, there were only fifteen distil-

MALT WHISKY CAKE

This recipe for a rich, moist malt whisky cake comes from Stewart Cameron, Executive Chef des Cuisines, and Derek Abbot, Chef de Cuisine, at the Turnberry Hotel in Ayrshire.

5 oz golden raisins	½ tsp salt
3 cups water	1 tsp nutmeg
12 Tbs butter	1 ½ Tbs lemon juice
1 ¼ cups sugar	1 cup finely chopped
3 large eggs	walnuts
5 oz flour	3 oz. single malt Scotch
1 tsp baking soda	

•Cover the raisins with water and simmer for fifteen minutes. Drain, setting aside two tablespoons of the liquid.

•Cream the butter and sugar, and beat in the eggs one at a time. Stir in the flour, which has been sifted with the baking soda, salt, and nutmeg. Add the liquid from the raisins. Then fold in the raisins, lemon juice, chopped walnuts, and whisky.

•Bake in a 9-inch round cake pan for thirty to forty minutes at 350 degrees Fahrenheit.

leries operating throughout Scotland, with several only operating on a part-time basis. In 1933, the Pot-still Malt Distillers Association of Scotland, the umbrella organization formed to serve all the Scotch malt whisky distilleries, even went so far as to recommend to its members that they not operate at all.

The real breakthrough for Scotch in the United States came after the Second World War, when American servicemen stationed in the United Kingdom returned home with a newly acquired taste. The demand they created boosted the sales of Scotch in the decades that followed, although the downside to this was that Scotch became rather too widely associated with the immediate post-war generation. As a result, Scotch soon came to be considered unfashionable by the young.

At home, the industry was taking a more outward look. The Scotch Whisky Association replaced the Pot-still Malt Distillers Association in 1942, with an eye to protecting and promoting the interest of the trade in general at home and abroad. The SWA continues to be the industry's trade association. With its head office in Edinburgh and its public affairs office in London, the SWA provides statistics for political lobbying and acts as a watchdog over the industry.

Throughout the 1950s and 1960s, successive British governments continued to increase taxation, and the industry's response was to form ever larger groupings.

Exploiting the Scots connection, salesmen and industry representatives throughout the world extolled the unmatched virtues of Scotch whisky.

By the 1970s, the Scotch industry faced a crisis. For far too long, Scotland's distilleries had relied upon their worldwide reputations to overcome competitive marketing. As in the days of the old clan feuds, the policy had always been to allow one brand to compete against another. It suddenly became apparent that the real competition was coming from elsewhere; in particular, from the cutthroat and new-look white spirit products, vodka in particular, aggressively marketed with a futuristic appeal. The Scotch whisky industry's immediate response was to panic. During the 1970s, overproduction and price-cutting caused havoc, culminating in the surplus "whisky lake" of 1980. Distilleries were mothballed pending an improvement in market demand. Only then did the industry's major figures realize that a new approach was not only inevitable, but overdue. For the first time, it dawned on them that they should pool their combined resources and work together. Thus it was agreed to place an emphasis on quality at appropriate costs. With the switch from volume to value came distinctive packaging that drew attention to the marvelous variety of different tastes and localities. The Scotch whisky industry was reborn. And while an increase in taxation levels during the 1980s led to a steady investment of overseas capital, the production of single malt

page 33: *A tranquil harbor scene on the Island of Islay.* above: *A distant view of the Paps of Jura from the Caol Ila Distillery on Islay.* right: *The Laphroaig Distillery gleams white in the morning sunshine.*

Scotch remains a profoundly Scottish industry. The European Community has decreed that a distilled spirit shall be recognized as genuine Scotch whisky only if it originated and was distilled in Scotland.

As part of its new marketing approach, the industry opened its distilleries to the public. In 1982, as a joint initiative with the industry, the Scottish Tourist Board launched the Scotch Whisky Trail and, following the example of the famous wine chateaux of France, Glenfiddich and Glenfarclas became the first distilleries to open their doors so that visitors could come and see for themselves how uisgebeatha was made. Other distilleries soon followed their example and opened specialized visitor centers to explain the sub-

tleties of single-malts; for example, United Distillers at Glenkinchie, Blair Athol, Royal Lochnagar, Cardhu, and Oban; and Campbell Distillers at Edradour. Two miles (3.2km) south of Forres, east of Inverness, is the old distillery of Dallas Dhu, closed in 1983, then reopened as a museum by Historic Scotland, a government-funded preservation agency, as an example of a traditional working Speyside distillery. At Aviemore, a popular holiday resort center south of Inverness, is the Cairngorm Whisky Centre and Museum, which stocks the largest selection of single-malts to be found anywhere.

The Scotch Whisky Heritage Centre can be found in Edinburgh, Scotland's capital, close to the entrance of Edinburgh Castle. Here visitors can take a ride in a whisky barrel for an audiovisual journey (available in six languages) through the centuries that provides a wealth of anecdotes and historical information regarding the Scotch industry.

Thanks to this new openness, many single-malts are no longer a connoisseur's secret. They now have an entirely new appeal. The public is encouraged to experiment, to learn the difference between the single-malts and the commercially popular blends. At

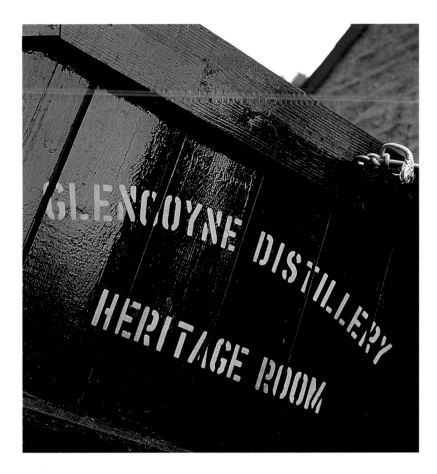 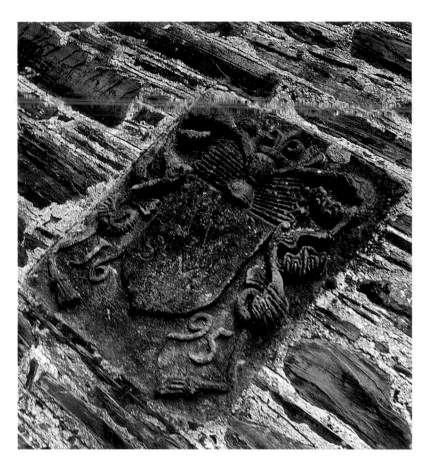

above left: *The entrance to the heritage Room at the Glengoyne Distillery, Dunbarton.* **above right:** *A coat of arms declares the antiquity of this distillery building.*

the same time, younger consumers have been targeted by ad campaigns showing the versatility of Scotch with mixers and in cocktails. Part of a taste for Scotch depends on the climate; the deep, dark single-malts of Campbeltown or Islay are more readily suited to chilly winter nights than hot, tropical sunshine. Yet with mixers and cocktails, and the breaking down of traditional snobberies about how Scotch should be drunk, habits are changing. Musty old traditions, while not entirely rejected, have been given a modern interpretation.

In the United States and Canada, the lighter colored blends, such as Dewars, J&B, Johnny Walker Black Label, Johnny Walker Red Label, Cutty Sark, Clan MacGregor, Passport, and Chivas Regal, have to date created the highest demand. The best-known and most popular single-malts in North America at this time are Glenfiddich and The Macallan, but as other brand names become increasingly available, and palates become more sophisticated, the market has been expanding quickly. The romantic image of Scotland and the Scots enhances this growth.

Today the Scotch whisky industry has become a truly international enterprise. This has been reflected in the creation of the Keepers of the Quaich, an exclusive society formed within the Scotch whisky industry to honor those who have served and helped to promote the interests of their industry worldwide. There are currently Keepers of the Quaich representing fifty-two countries, and each summer and autumn banquets and enrollment ceremonies are held at the society's headquarters, Blair Castle in Perthshire. Among those who have been named honorary Keepers of the Quaich in recent years are Ronald Reagan, fortieth president of the United States, Casper Weinberger, the former U.S. secretary of state, and the Prince of Wales.

opposite: *At the end of a day of whisky-making, the courtyard at the Fettercairn Distillery is hosed down in preparation for the next day's exertions. In this double exposure, the image of a Fettercairn still is suspended like a ghost before the sunset.* above: *Taps and handles at the Oban Distillery in Argyll.*

2

The Art of DISTILLING

The basic steps of distillation are the same wherever it takes place. They comprise

nine stages: steeping, germinating, kilning, milling, mashing, fermentation, distilla-

tion, cask filling, and maturation.

Ingredients   There are two ingredients to Scotch: barley and water. The barley comes from the fertile lands of mainland Scotland, for the most part. Distilleries are always located near water, and in the Highlands of Scotland there is an abundance of mountain streams, known as burns, and many great, fast flowing rivers. By combining malted barley and Scottish water with the richly scented smoke of a peat fire, you have the basic ingredients for single-malt Scotch. After that, everything else is magic.

The Process   To begin with, the barley is soaked in water for two or three days, then spread out on a concrete floor to germinate. The barley is turned at regular intervals, usually by hand, and after seven days it changes into what is called green malt. This green malt is transferred to a kiln to be dried and to halt the process of germination. The kiln has a perforated floor to allow the hot air and smoke from a furnace below to circulate through the grain. In Scotch whisky-making, it is usually the custom to add peat to the furnace, which gives the whisky its unique, smoky flavor.

When the malt is dry, it is transferred into sacks or wooden bins, where it remains for several weeks. After that, it is taken to be crushed into a meal called grist, which resembles a coarse flour. This grist is then ground between two pairs of steel rollers before being moved into a grist hopper.

From the grist hopper, the grist is mixed with hot water in the mash tun, a large, circular metal vessel. As the mixture is stirred by revolving rakes, a sweet liquid called wort is drawn off through perforated floor plates and pumped through a cooler into a fermentation vessel called the washback.

As there are still sugars remaining in the mash tun, a second and third flush of water takes place before the remaining draff is removed and transported off to be used as cattle food.

opposite: *The grist grinder at the Bowmore Distillery on the Island of Islay.* **above:** *Washbacks at the Bowmore Distillery.*

A waste energy recovery system serves the local community by providing hot air to heat the local swimming pool.

above: *Distillery workers at the Glengoyne Distillery, Scotland's most southerly Highland distillery.*   opposite and pages 45–46: *The stills at Glenmorangie Distillers tower 16 feet 10 inches (330.5cm) high.*

Washbacks are usually manufactured from pine or larch. Once they have been filled, a measured amount of yeast is added to the wort, causing it to froth as the yeast consumes the sugar in the wort and converts it to alcohol and carbon dioxide. Fermentation takes place over a couple of days, and the wort is transformed into wash, a weak form of alcohol, creamy brown in color. This is then pumped into the wash charger, which acts as a holding vessel.

Pot stills are like vast copper kettles. Their basic shape has remained the same since Scotch whisky was first created, although their individual shapes can be remarkably different. No two distilleries use identical pot stills, and the shape undoubtedly does influence the individuality of the final product, although nobody can actually explain why.

Once the wash has passed from the wash charger into the wash still, the wash is heated until it boils and steam rises up the still. As it passes through the worm, a spiral copper tube immersed in a vat of cold water, the alcohol and water in the vapor once again condense into liquid.

Since alcohol is vaporized more readily than water, this liquid, called low wines, is much higher in alcohol than the wash. From the low wines receiver the liquid runs into the spirit receiver for the second distillation process.

Once more the low wines are heated to the point of separation. The alcoholic vapors are condensed and cooled and the spirit is run off. All the low wines and spirit are run off through the spirit sample safe, which is operated by the stillman.

From this point Customs & Excise requires all spirit to be kept under lock and key. When the low wines passes through the spirit sample safe, the stillman records the temperature, and then measures the strength by using a hydrometer floating within a testing jar inside the safe.

The spirit from the distillation in the spirit still is then split into three parts. Once the middle cut or "heart of the run" is identified as being the required strength and quality for malt whisky, the first and final parts of the run, making up the larger proportion, are sent back to the low wines vessel for distillation again.

tained in each cask is by deducting the unfilled weight from the filled weight.

Having been filled and weighed, therefore, casks are marked and stored in bonded warehouses where, by law, they must remain for a minimum of three years. Only then are they permitted to be removed for blending purposes.

The longer a single-malt matures, the better the quality of the whisky in the bottle. Some distilleries retain single-malts for up to thirty years before releasing them onto the marketplace. With the smoothness of silk upon the palate, it is hardly surprising that they should be considered the equivalent of liquid gold.

Types of Single Malt Whiskies, Blends, Grain Whisky, and De Luxe Blends   The purpose of the distillation process is to produce a single malt product. However, until the mid-eighteenth century, single malt whisky had a limited appeal to the general public. It was considered too strong and too intoxicating for the average taste.

In the meantime, the middle cut is passed to an oak vessel known as the intermediate spirit receiver. From here it is pumped to the spirit receiver located in the filling store. Scottish distilleries make only two distillations, one distillation in the wash still and a second in the spirit still. (The one exception is Auchentoshan at Clydebank, which together with Irish distilleries operates a triple-distillation system.)

By this stage, the spirit is now clear in color with a strength of between 70 and 75 percent alcohol by volume (123 to 131 proof). By adding water, the strength is then reduced to maturation strength, approximately 64 percent alcohol by volume (112 proof). The spirit is now ready for what is often called the Sleep, where it is placed in oak casks and left to mature.

The Cask   Casks are made from top-quality oak, and are acquired by distilleries secondhand from the United States, Spain, and Portugal. The majority of these casks have been used previously for maturing bourbon whiskey or sherry, and the wood, which has absorbed a certain amount of these products, plays a significant part in the coloring of the mature single malt whisky.

Casks are weighed before and after filling. Every cask is manufactured by hand, so weights vary considerably. Because of this the only accurate method of determining the amount of spirit con-

above: *Angus Macaulay, stillman at the Lagavulin Distillery.* **below:** *Fitting rings at the Speyside Cooperage.* **opposite:** *Used casks awaiting treament at the Lagavulin Cooperage on the Island of Islay.*

above: *Every cask of Scotch whisky is stencilled with the distillery's name and other information so that it can be identified at any time.*

opposite: *Stencilling discs and samples at the Lagavulin distillery.*

At the same time, a considerable amount of competition sprang up from grain whisky manufacturers who were mixing barley with other cereals and making a light, extremely appealing alternative to Scotch whisky.

The two production processes are not dissimilar. Grain whisky is manufactured by transforming cereal starch into sugar, then into alcohol through fermentation and distillation.

However, this wasn't practiced to any great extent before the mid-nineteenth century, and what made it possible was the invention of a still that was internally heated by steam. This enabled continuous distillation to take place, whereas the traditional pot still needed to be repeatedly emptied and refilled.

The process of continuous distillation was being developed with some success in 1830 by Robert Stein, a prominent Scottish distiller, when Aeneas Coffey, a Dublin-based exciseman, took things one step further. He patented the concept and began marketing "Coffey's Continuous Patent Stills." Suddenly distillers found

top: *Ian "Pinky" Macarthur, warehouse supervisor at Lagavulin, holding a wine thief, used to sample the spirit.*   **above:** *Casks are laid out of doors to await collection.*   **opposite:** *Outside the Dalwhinnie Distillery, holding tanks containing water from the distillery supply.*

above: *Pot stills at the Laphroaig Distillery on the Island of Islay.* **opposite:** *The unusually squat and tall shape of the pot stills at Glenmorangie is instantly recognizable.*

SALAD OF RED AND BLACK FRUITS

(also known as Salade Stendahl *or* Salade Rouge et Noir*)*

"I feel that the choice of single-malt is extremely important [for this recipe]. The Macallan is, in my opinion, perfect for this," says J. Gordon McIntyre, proprietor of the Clifton House Hotel, where this delightful dessert may be savored. "Personally I don't think that it needs any cream, but, if anything, then add, beaten together, half-whipped double cream, half crème fraîche, a little sugar, and a glass of The Macallan all beaten together."

•Wash and pick over equal quantities, about one pound each, of fresh raspberries, red currants, brambles, dark plums, black grapes, strawberries, and blackberries. Take another pound each of raspberries and red currants and, in a blender, blend them together with a cup of sugar, three good measures of The Macallan, and some vanilla extract. Pour over the remaining fruits, cover tightly with plastic wrap, and allow to macerate at least overnight.

themselves able to produce a light whisky with popular appeal cheaply and efficiently, and the industry expanded rapidly.

Grain whisky is manufactured with malted barley, whole grain (corn or wheat), and yeast. Whole grain is cooked under pressure and added to the previously milled mash in a mash tun to convert the starch in both the malt and other cereals into a wort-sugar solution. This is cooled and pumped to washbacks where, with the addition of yeast, fermentation occurs.

The fermented wort, or wash, is pumped into Coffey stills for continuous distillation. As with single-malt production, the spirit created is passed into casks for maturation.

above: *Stout oak doors protect the malt deposit rooms from unwanted intruders.* **opposite:** *Original records and accounts are on display at the Dalmore Distillery in Speyside.*

above: *The spirit safe at the Glenmorangie Distillery. Only the exciseman is permitted to open the spirit safe.* **opposite:** *The wash condenser at the Glenturret Distillery in Perthshire.*

opposite: *A level view of a mash tun.* **above left:** *Inside of the mash tun at the Caol Ila Distillery on the Island of Islay.*

above right: *The head mash man at Lagavulin Distillery on Islay.*

Nothing is wasted in the Scotch whisky industry. Grain whisky is produced cheaply and in bulk, and 30 percent of the original grain is recovered after the distillation process and sold for use as animal feed.

From the 1850s onward, the growth of the Scotch whisky industry escalated. Andrew Usher, an agent for the Glenlivet, began experimenting with a selection of malt and grains, and the first blended whisky with popular appeal was created. The term blend was only used at first to describe a mixture of single-malts, but these are now known as vatted malts. Today a blend is a mix of single-malt with grain whisky. A de luxe whisky is a superior quality of blend, generally containing a higher quantity of older, mature malt. Some de luxe whiskies carry an age statement that refers to the youngest component in the bottle.

However, the majority of the world-famous names in Scotch whisky today are blends consisting of up to fifty different single-malt and grain whiskies. It is extraordinary how in addition to the unique individuality of each single-malt, an entire range of subtly blended Scotch whiskies can also hold its own so effortlessly on the international markets.

Chillfiltering Until recently, all Scotch whisky was produced without chillfiltering. As a result, it was prone to lose clarity with a change in temperature or when it had been exposed to air for a period, becoming cloudy or opaque in the bottle.

From a marketing point of view this was a drawback. After a considerable amount of research, chillfiltering was widely introduced to remove the proteins that cause the discoloration.

Although this proved to be a popular change, there are those who hold that by extracting these proteins, the heart of the whisky is destroyed and the original style changed. It is purely a matter of taste. A few brand names now proudly announce that they are unchillfiltered, but the majority remain chillfiltered.

Irish Whiskey, Japanese Whiskey, and Bourbon Whiskey Attempts have been made to copy Scotch whisky the

opposite: *Cask measuring tools.*   above: *Tools for the malt floor at the Balvenie Distillery, Speyside.*

page 64: *A golden measure of single malt Scotch whisky; what could be more inviting?*

world over, and although some of the spirits created are hard to fault, none exactly match the genuine product. Single malt Scotch and its subsequent blends are unique to Scotland.

Ireland once boasted a flourishing grain distillery industry, but only a handful of single-malts and blends are still produced. The Bushmills Distillery in County Antrim was licensed in 1608, making it the oldest licensed malt distillery in the world, although its single-malt was only released to the general public in the mid-1980s. The oldest malt available from the Emerald Isle comes from Coleraine, and the youngest to date from Tyrconnell Distillery at Cooley, near the mountains of Mourne. Note that whisky from Ireland (or, indeed, anywhere but Scotland) is spelled whiskey, with an "e".

Irish distilleries use a triple-distillation process that involves three pot stills, and the spirit consequently undergoes a third distillation before passing through the spirit sample safe.

The story of the Japanese whiskey industry dates back to the early part of the twentieth century, when a young Japanese student named Taketsuru enrolled at Glasgow University and went on to train with Mackie & Co. (the makers of White Horse) in Glasgow and Speyside. Upon his return to Japan, he helped develop the giant Suntory empire, then formed the Nikka Distillery.

The first bourbon whiskey was distilled in 1789 by a Baptist clergyman, the Reverend Elijah Craig, a Scotsman, who settled at Royal Spring on the Georgetown Creek in Georgetown, Kentucky. Bourbon whiskey, a corn-based spirit, is notably sweet and robust and gains some of its typical character from the caramel flavors that are a natural component of the wood in which it is left to mature. Because of this, bourbon whiskey must be aged only in new casks. In a nice twist, this means that old bourbon whiskey casks are sold to Scottish distilleries, where the cask-wood serves to enhance the eventual coloring of the single-malt.

TRADITIONAL SCOTTISH HAGGIS

Alan Hill is the Executive Director of Food and Beverage at Gleneagles Hotel, in Auchterarder, Perthshire, one of the most famous hotel resorts in the world. When Hill and his staff prepare haggis, they don't hold back: the following recipe will yield forty 2 ½-pound haggises. At right, a haggis is served with clapshot lamb, bashed neeps, and champit tatties.

50 lbs lamb offal (heart, lungs, liver)	2 ½ lbs salt
7 ½ lbs beef fat	1 lb black ground pepper
7 ½ lbs kidney fat	30 lbs lamb stock
2 ½ lbs chopped onions	40 prepared sheep stomachs or
30 lbs pinhead oatmeal	artificial casings

•Cover the lamb offal with water and bring to a boil. Cook for ninety minutes, or until the lamb is well cooked. Remove and let cool.

• Mince the beef fat and kidney fat through a medium blade food mill and place in a mixing bowl.

•Put the cooked offal through the food mill. Add to the fat and thoroughly mix together. Add the onions, pinhead oatmeal, and seasoning, and once again thoroughly mix together.

•Gradually add the lamb stock until the correct consistency has been reached for piping into the sheep's stomach or artificial casings. Using a large pastry bag or sausage stuffer, fill the stomachs or casings and cut to the required size.

•Place the sealed haggis into cold salted water and bring to a boil. Simmer for one hour and allow to cool. The haggis will be reheated for serving later.

3

A Whisky Tour of **SCOTLAND**

Scotland spreads over approximately 30,411 square miles (78,764.5sq km)

of territory, with land as diverse as the rich, rolling farmland of the south-

ern borders with England; the lush coastal plains of the east against the

North Sea; the harsh, spectacular mountains and glens of the remote

Highlands; and, off the western coastline, the gem-like scattered islands of

the Inner and Outer Hebrides.

page 66: *A view of sunlit meadowland on Speyside.* page 67: *A misty sunrise over the Strathisla Distillery on Speyside.* above: *Rich farmland sweeps along beside the course of the River Spey in the Highlands of Scotland.* opposite: *Nearly half of the distilleries in Scotland are concentrated in the area called Speyside, with the remainder scattered throughout the land.*

Scotland occupies the northern 37 percent of the main British Isles, and while it is a tiny country, it is one with a distinct sense of identity. While the Romans, the Saxons, and the Normans successfully invaded England and Wales, they did not succeed in conquering Scotland, although the Romans did try to establish themselves as far north as Perth, and the Normans arrived peaceably in the reign of David I. England fared little better in imposing its will on its northern neighbor until the two countries united under a Scottish king in 1603.

But Scotland was never an easy realm to govern. While Edinburgh, in the southeast, consolidated its reputation as the ancient center for law and administration, Glasgow, in the southwest, expanded into Scotland's commercial and industrial heartbeat. While this was taking place, the Highlands—everything north

of a range of hills stretching from coast-to-coast above the two cities, and loosely called the Highland Line—were very much left to their own devices.

It was within this Highland region that Scotch whisky distilling prospered, and continues to prosper, serving the country's growing urban communities. However, there have been successful Lowland distilleries, as well, and it is these that we will consider first.

THE LOWLANDS, THE LIGHTEST OF THE BREED

South of the Highland line there was once a number of distilleries, but those that remain in Edinburgh, Glasgow, Dumbarton, Girvan, and in the Kingdom of Fife are for the most part concerned with grain distilling, blending, and bottling. There are only two remaining

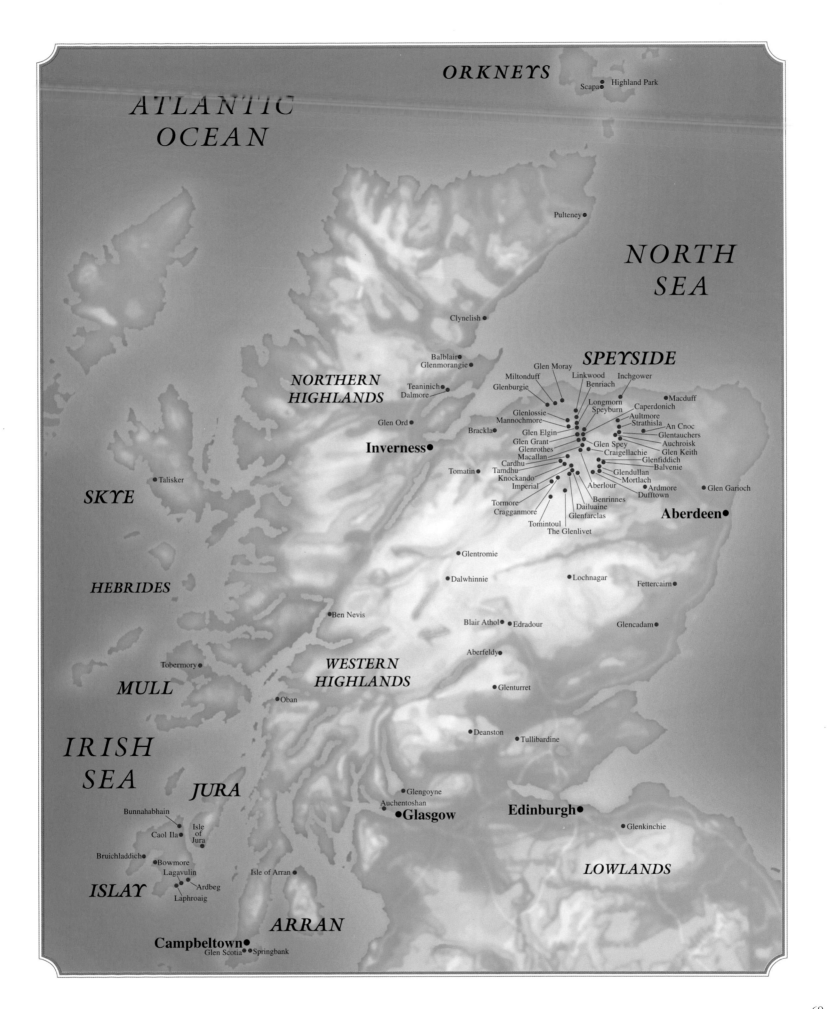

ORKNEYS

Scapa • • Highland Park

ATLANTIC
OCEAN

NORTH
SEA

Pulteney •

Clynelish •

Balblair •
Glenmorangie •

NORTHERN
HIGHLANDS

Teaninich • •
Dalmore

SPEYSIDE

Glen Moray •
Miltonduff • Linkwood • Inchgower •
Glenburgie • Benriach •

Longmorn • Caperdonich •
Speyburn • • Macduff
Glenlossie • Aultmore •
Mannochmore • Strathisla • An Cnoc
Glen Elgin • Glentauchers •
Glen Grant • Glen Spey • Auchroisk •
Glenrothes • Craigellachie • Glen Keith •
Macallan • Glenfiddich •
Cardhu • Glendullan • Balvenie •
Tamdhu • Mortlach •
Knockando • Aberlour • Ardmore • • Glen Garioch
Imperial • Benrinnes • Dufftown •

Glen Ord •

Brackla •

Inverness •

Tomatin •
Tomintoul •

SKYE

Talisker •

HEBRIDES

Glentromie •

Dalwhinnie •

Lochnagar •

Fettercairn •

Aberdeen •

Tormore •
Cragganmore •
Tomintoul •
Dailuaine •
Glenfarclas •
The Glenlivet •

Ben Nevis •

Blair Athol • • Edradour

Glencadam •

WESTERN
HIGHLANDS

Aberfeldy •

Tobermory •

MULL

Oban •

Glenturret •

Deanston • • Tullibardine

IRISH
SEA

JURA

Glengoyne •
Auchentoshan •
Glasgow •

Edinburgh •

Bunnahabhain •

Caol Ila •

Isle
of
Jura

Bruichladdich •
• Bowmore
Lagavulin •
• Ardbeg
Laphroaig

Isle of Arran •

ISLAY

Glenkinchie •

LOWLANDS

ARRAN

Campbeltown •
Glen Scotia • • Springbank

69

operational single-malt distilleries classified as Lowland, although there is always the chance that somebody might open up another or reopen an older one.

DUNBARTONSHIRE

Although this region has mountains in the north between Loch Lomond and Loch Long, the lower district alongside the Clyde Estuary is flat and heavily industrial as it approaches the sprawling mass of the city of Glasgow to the east.

Clydebank

This industrial town, ten miles (16.1km) northwest of Glasgow, on the northern banks of the River Clyde, was once farmland until it was transformed in 1871 into one of the world's great ship-building yards. From Clydebank were launched such famous ocean-going liners as the *Lusitania*, the *Queen Mary*, and the *QE2*.

Auchentoshan Auchentoshan Distillery dates from the early 1800s. Crouching in front of a large man-made lake, with a backdrop of high-rise buildings, this is certainly not the most aesthetically pleasing of Scotland's distilleries, but it does have character, having been largely rebuilt after suffering wartime bomb damage. This is the only distillery in Scotland to use triple-distillation, and the malt, bottled between ten and twenty-one years old, is light and clean-tasting.

EAST LOTHIAN

On the south side of the Firth of Forth, this old county, formerly known as Haddingtonshire, is fringed to the south by the Lammermuir Hills. Very much an agricultural community inland, there are fishing villages along its coast.

Pencaitland

A pretty little village, Pencaitland lies amid rich farming country-side and close to the market town of Haddington. The Tyne Water flows through the village under a stone bridge that dates from 1510.

Glenkinchie Southeast of Edinburgh, near the village of Pencaitland in East Lothian, is the Glenkinchie Distillery. It was started by a local farmer in the 1830s, but subsequently used for twenty-five years as a sawmill before being turned back into a distillery again. Barley is grown locally, and the water is taken from the Kinchie Burn, which flows through the distillery from the gentle Lammermuir Hills on its way to the River Tyne. The Glenkinchie single-malt, a dry, clean dram, is bottled at ten years, and is one of the six "classic malts" selected by United Distillers.

The floor maltings at Glenkinchie were closed in 1968, but the equipment remains on show as part of the Museum of Malt Whisky Production. With the closure in 1994 of the Bladnoch Distillery in Wigtownshire, Glenkinchie is currently the southernmost Lowland distillery.

CAMPBELTOWN, THE LOST KINGDOM OF SCOTCH WHISKY

This settlement on the southernmost tip of the Mull of Kintyre, the sliver of land that snakes down Scotland's west coast between

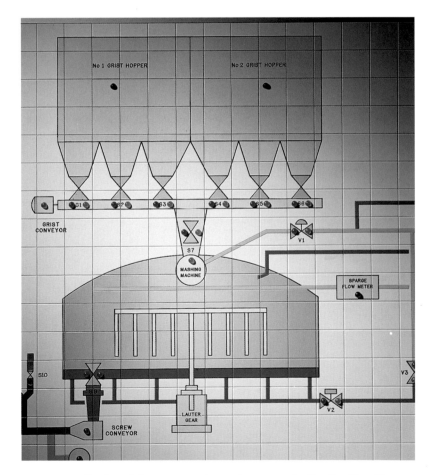

opposite: *Dark and fascinating, the wash tuns at the Cardhu Distillery on Speyside.* **above:** *Modern electrical systems at the Glenkinchie Distillery make it possible to monitor the entire production process at each step.*

above left: *Electrical circuits need to be constantly checked to ensure that everything runs smoothly.*   above right: *The powerhouse and control boards at the Glenmorangie Distillery.*   opposite: *The tasting room at the Macallan Distillery.*

the Kilbrannon Sound and the Sound of Gigha on the Atlantic Ocean, was once considered to be the Whisky Capital of Scotland. Local supplies of peat and barley were abundant, and there was a relatively inexpensive source of coal nearby. With more than thirty distilleries operating toward the end of the nineteenth century, it is no wonder that a popular music hall song should have been named after Campbeltown Loch.

Alas, the coal supply was soon used up, and as bottling at too young an age made the quality of the whisky suffer, the local industry went into decline. Today, although Campbeltown retains its own Customs & Excise classification, only two distilleries continue to operate.

Glen Scotia   The Glen Scotia distillery was built in 1832, and it remains privately owned to this day. Although it is currently not in full production, there is some talk of firing up the stills once again. The rich, salty single-malt, bottled at twelve, fourteen, and sixteen years, is available.

Springbank   Founded in the 1820s by the Mitchell family, who once operated a local illicit still and whose descendants continue to retain control, Springbank Distillery is the great Campbeltown survivor. This is one of the very few remaining distilleries to bottle its products on site, and the mellow single-malt, bottled at twelve, fifteen, twenty-one, twenty-five, and thirty years, is not chillfiltered.

Longrow, bottled at between sixteen and twenty-one years, is also produced at Springbank Distillery, although the name is taken from a Campbeltown distillery that closed in the last century. Using only peat-dried barley, this is a strong-tasting single-malt with a very traditional, almost medicinal flavor.

SPEYSIDE, THE HEART OF WHISKY COUNTRY

The River Spey rises eight miles (12.9km) east of the end of Loch Lochy, and flows east and northeast through Inverness-shire and Morayshire, and along the border of Banffshire to the Moray Firth at Kingston, between the seaside towns of Lossiemouth and

above: *Turning the malt at the Balvenie Distillery.*   below: *Pagoda style roof towers are a feature throughout Scotland's distilleries.*

Portnockie. It is the most rapid river in Scotland and travels 107 miles (172.2km), and hence the area through which it passes has generally come to be known as Speyside.

With five other great rivers and an abundance of burn and river water, rain, and winter snow from the Monadhliath and Cairngorm mountains, this region was known in olden times as The Drowned Land. On the southern shore of the Moray Firth, prime pasture and farmland is blessed with a mild and predictable climate. And with the added bonus of fields of barley and rich deposits of peat, it is hardly surprising that forty-one distilleries should spring up alongside the rivers Spey, Findhorn, Lossie, Avon, Fiddich, and Livet. With its great concentration of single-malt manufacturers, and its historical importance as the scene of many a confrontation between illicit distiller, smuggler, and exciseman, Speyside can easily be called the heart of Scotch whisky country.

Much of the region's distinction as a manufacturer of uisge-beatha derived from The Glenlivet, at Ballindalloch, the first distillery to apply for a license under legislation that was introduced in 1824 to help what was by then an industry in danger of slipping out of control. At the time there were more than one hundred illicit stills known to be operating in the vicinity, The Glenlivet, although an illegal product, had become an established name to the

extent that it was even enjoyed by King George IV during the course of his visit to Edinburgh in 1822.

Given its association with quality and excellence, it was not long before The Glenlivet's name was hijacked by more than twenty other neighboring distilleries, only four of which could actually claim to be located in the glen. In 1880 a lawsuit and settlement firmly established that there was only one original Glenlivet, although for traditional reasons use of the name is still permitted as a hyphenated addition.

Distilleries, along with agriculture, are the backbone of Speyside's economy today. They pop up around virtually every corner of every country road, features of the landscape, their single-malts each reflecting a contrasting subtle aspect of this fertile corner of Scotland.

NAIRNSHIRE

The River Nairn and River Findhorn flow through this country on the Moray Firth, with the highland capital of Inverness to the west. Agriculture, fishing, and distilleries are the main sources of work, although tourism has been growing rapidly.

Cawdor

Its ancient castle still intact and open to the public, this village five and a half miles (8.8km) southwest of the town of Nairn is inevitably associated with William Shakespeare's Macbeth. Nearby,

SADDLE OF VENISON ON POTATO GALETTES WITH MINTED JUNIPER SAUCE

Deer have always been plentiful in the Highlands of Scotland, and venison is one of the favorite game meats at the Scotsman's table. What follows is Alan Hill's unique way of preparing venison fillets for guests at the Gleneagles resort hotel.

Serves 4

4 6-oz fillets of
    Scottish venison
salt and pepper
1 Tbs oil
3 Tbs butter
1 cup crushed
    juniper berries
2 oz gin
4 oz port

1 ½ cup game gravy
2 tsp Arran mustard
2 Tbs rowan jelly
½ oz mint, julienned
4 potato galettes
    (see recipe below)
200g spinach leaves, sauteed
4 Tbs butter to finish

•Season and saute the fillets of venison to taste in a touch of hot oil and butter. Remove, dry, and keep warm.

•Discard any excess fat from the cooking pan, deglaze with the gin and port, and reduce by one half.

•Add the game gravy and the crushed juniper berries and further reduce by one half, then pass through a fine sieve and return to the stove.

•Reheat the potato galettes and place into the center of a serving plate.

•Add the mint, Arran mustard, and a touch of rowan jelly to the sauce, then check the consistency and seasoning.

•Quickly whisk the butter into the sauce and place several tablespoons around each of the potato galettes.

•Place one of the fillets of venison on each of the galettes, garnish with the spinach, and serve hot immediately.

POTATO GALETTES

2 lbs boiled and pureed potatoes
salt and pepper
2 Tbs butter
1 tsp nutmeg
2 oz chopped herbs (sage, thyme, parsley)
3 Tbs flour

Method

•Place the potatoes in a saucepan and cook any excess moisture off. Beat in the butter and season well with salt, pepper, and nutmeg. Add the chopped herbs and allow to cook for 10 minutes.

•On a lightly floured surface, roll out the potatoes into a cylinder shape approximately 4 inches in diameter and cut into disks approximately ½-inch thick.

opposite: *A bottle of the Glenlivet 12-year-old, famous for centuries.* **above:** *The spirit safe, where the stillman can first taste the raw whisky for quality. It is kept locked under the watchful eye of the customs and exciseman.*

surrounded by hills, open fields, and pine woods, the River Findhorn flows its gentle course across this coastal plain toward the Moray Firth.

Royal Brackia

A malt brew-house existed on the Cawdor estate before 1812, when the current distillery was built. This was the first distillery to receive a Royal Warrant of Appointment, first as supplier to King William IV in 1835, then to Queen Victoria in 1838. Closed for a short period, the distillery reopened in 1990. While most of the output goes toward blending, the single-malt is bottled at ten years.

MORAY

This low, coastal region is divided by gentle hills rising to the mountains on its southern border. Fertile valleys and forest acres are bisected by the rivers Lossie, Spey, Avon, and Livet.

above: *During the late summer and autumn, Scotland has some of the most spectacular sunsets to be seen anywhere. Here the day draws to an end over Nairn, in Morayshire.*

THE CLIFTON HOUSE

J. Gordon McIntyre runs the Clifton House Hotel, in Nairn, in a very particular way, and whatever else may be said of him, he runs his hotel with style. He has lived at Clifton House for all of his sixty-six years, and has opened it up for guests since his father died in 1952. He can remember the time when there was no electricity in the Clifton House, and the warm light of oil lamps and candles suffused the house with romance and mystery.

McIntyre's house reflects his personality; it is filled with evidence of his love of color, music, flowers, books, pictures, and theater. A stay in this extremely unusual house always provokes a strong and immediate reaction: most people feel totally, instantly at home, warmed, cosseted, and relaxed; but some quickly begin to feel claustrophobic and stifled, and are hellbent on escape at the first possible opportunity.

If you must live with a telephone, if you don't particularly care about what you eat, and if you don't care if you never drink wine, then Gordon suggests you save your money and go elsewhere.

above: *A bottle of The Macallan, a single malt whisky renowned the world over.*

Forress

This prosperous market town sits between the glacial mounds of the Cluny Hills and the shoreline fossil cliff that looks onto the Moray Firth. The ancient Highland clan of Brodie has its ancestral seats here, and nearby is Darnaway Castle, visited by Mary Queen of Scots in 1564.

Glenburgie   East of Alves, this distillery was founded on the site of an illicit still in 1829, closed and revived in 1878, and enlarged in 1958. Much of its product goes to blending. The single-malt bottling age varies, but is reported to be eight years, and is largely exported.

Elgin

The town of Elgin is thirty-seven miles (59.9km) from Inverness, and is home to the ruins of a cathedral founded in 1224. Situated on a promontory of land above the low-lying River Lossie, it is inland from Lossiemouth, which once served as its seaport.

Benriach   The Benriach Distillery lies on the Elgin-to-Rothes road and takes its water from the River Lossie. Dating from the end of the nineteenth century, it was closed in 1903 and reopened sixty-five years later. It still retains its hand-turned malting floor, and the single-malt is bottled at ten years.

opposite: *A bottle of the Balvenie, from a distillery owned by the same family for five generations.* **above:** *For centuries, strange looking implements have been used to check whisky quality in the testing room at the Cardhu Distillery.*

SCOTCH TRUFFLES

This recipe for delicious chocolate truffles flavored with single malt Scotch comes from J. Gordon McIntyre, of the Clifton House Hotel. Use the very best dark chocolate and a good single malt whisky. A Speyside is ideal, or a Glenmorangie, but definitely not one of the Islay malts, which for this purpose are too smoky.

    1 lb dark chocolate broken into small pieces

    9 Tbs double cream

    1 tsp vanilla extract

    2 oz single malt whisky

    grated chocolate, or chocolate powder, or chopped
        nuts, in which to roll the truffles.

•Melt the chocolate very gently in a double boiler. In a separate saucepan, heat the cream until it is very hot but not boiling. Add the cream to the chocolate as soon as it has melted, and remove from the heat. Add the vanilla and the malt whisky, combine thoroughly, and stir occasionally until the mixture begins to cool.

•Beat the mixture until it lightens in color and then set aside to allow it to become workably firm. Take a spoonful of the mixture and roll it in the sugar or chocolate mixture. Set on a tray lightly dusted with chocolate powder and place in a refrigerator or freezer until it becomes firm. When cold and firm, store in the refrigerator in a container with a tightly fitting lid.

Glen Elgin   The Glen Elgin Distillery at Longmorn, south of the town of Elgin, was built in 1890. Water is obtained from the springs in Glen Rothes, and although much of the single-malt is used for blending, a certain amount is bottled at twelve years, at present mainly for the Japanese market.

Glenlossie   In close proximity to the River Lossie, in the Lossie Valley, this distillery dates from 1876. In 1962, the stills were increased from four to six, and a new mash was introduced in 1992. Glenlossie single-malt is bottled at ten years.

Glen Moray   Converted from a brewery in 1897, the Glenmoray-Glenlivet Distillery, located in town, was greatly expanded in 1958, when it dropped the Glenlivet affix. The single-malt is bottled at twelve years.

Linkwood   A prominent local family built this distillery in the 1820s, setting it in the woods beside the Linkwood Burn. It was pulled down and rebuilt in 1872, closed and then reopened in 1902 when great emphasis was placed on not disturbing any aspect of the environment, not even a spider's web. In 1962, the distillery was again rebuilt, with exact replications of the original stills and layout. Linkwood single-malt is bottled at twelve years.

Longmorn   The name of this distillery comes from the Gaelic "Lhangmorn," which means Morgan the Holy Man, and it stands on the site of a former chapel. Both the water for production and the peat used for the furnace are gathered from the nearby Mannoch Hills. The single-malt is bottled at twelve and fifteen years.

Mannochmore   This distillery was built on part of the Glenlossie Distillery site and draws process water from the Bardon Burn, which flows from the Mannoch Hills with cooling water from the Gedloch Burns and the Burn of the Foths. The distillery also operates three farms, Glenlossie, Easterton, and Wardend, producing its own barley.

Most of the whisky goes toward blending, but the single-malt is bottled at twelve years.

Miltonduff   Built on the original site of an illicit still and legalized in 1824, the Miltonduff-Glenlivet Distillery stands close to the

above *Pot stills vary in size and height throughout the distilleries of Scotland. Certainly this has some effect on the taste and quality of the final product, making every single-malt subtly different.*

ruins of Pluscarden Abbey, which dates from 1230. Water is taken from the Black Burn running from the peaty slopes of the Black Hill. The Miltonduff single-malt is bottled at twelve years.

Rothes

The town of Rothes, nine miles (14.5km) southeast of Elgin, lies close to the River Spey and consists of one main street behind which, on either side, are located its five distilleries.

A pipe that carried whisky for blending between the Glen Grant and Caperdonich distilleries used to span the main street at its north end; when the pipe was dismantled during the 1960s,

workers discovered a number of plugged holes, indicating that over the years locals had attempted—perhaps with some success—to siphon off whisky.

Caperdonich   The distillery takes its name from a well and was first operated in 1897 as a second-stage developer for the Glen Grant Distillery, to which, as mentioned above, it was linked by a pipe across the main road. This short-lived operation ended in 1901, and it was not until 1965 that the distillery was rebuilt and refurbished for production again, taking the Caperdonich name. Most of the single-malt produced goes into Seagram blends,

above: *A view of the new warehouse at the Macallan Distillery on Speyside.* **opposite:** *The storage room in the Macallan Cooperage.*

opposite: *In this elegant tasting room the Lang Brothers, of Glasgow, create some of the world's finest blended whiskies.*   above: *The Glenfiddich Distillery, originally built by the Grant family in Dufftown in 1887.*

although the Caperdonich single-malt is sometimes found as an independent bottling.

Glen Grant

Two brothers built the Glen Grant Distillery in the town of Rothes in 1840, and it was to remain with their descendants until l931. The Glen Grant Burn provides a ready supply of water, and it is said that the distillery's attractive park and orchard are inhabited by tiny fairies who, alas, only make themselves visible to true believers.

Glen Grant single-malt is bottled at between five and ten years, and occasionally at other ages.

Glenrothes

The Glenrothes Distillery was built in 1878 on the site of an old sawmill, and has expanded considerably in recent years. Although a large percentage of the single-malt goes toward blending, it is also bottled and available at twelve and fifteen years.

Located at the distillery is the Cutty Sark Visitor Centre, which tells the story of one of the world's most popular Scotch blends.

Glen Spey

Glen Spey was built in 1885 to mill cereals, but its owner soon discovered that distilling was a more profitable operation, although he sold the distillery to the gin-manufacturing Gilbey brothers within two years of starting. After a number of takeovers, this distillery was entirely rebuilt in 1970, and virtually all of what is currently produced goes toward blending. However, a small amount of single-malt is bottled at eight years.

Speyburn Known locally as "The Gibbet" because of its location to "Cnock na Croich," which translates from the Gaelic as "Hill of the Gibbet," this handsome Victorian distillery of two and three-story buildings sits against a wooded hillside. Water is taken from the hills of the Glen of Rothes, and although most of the produce is used for blending, the single-malt is bottled at ten years.

Carron

This village, which is nestled below Carron Hill, is located on the Lower Spey, six miles (9.7km) southwest of the Rock of Craigellachie.

Dailuaine Erected in 1852 under the shadow of Ben Rinnes, Dailuaine means "The Green Vale" in Gaelic. Major reconstruction took place in 1960, with the number of pot stills increased to six, the introduction of a mechanical coal-stoking system, and the conversion of floor maltings to a Saladin box system. Process water is

left: The striking waterfront of the Laphoraig Distillery on the Island of Islay. above: The Glenlivet Distillery on Speyside has a streamlined, modern look. opposite: The Laphroaig Distillery is set on a bay on the southern shore of the Island of Islay and dates back to 1815.

drawn from the Bailliemullich Burn, cooling water from the Carron Burn, and malting steeping water comes from the Burn of Derrybeg. All three of these streams originate on Ben Rinnes. Dailuaine single-malt is bottled at sixteen years.

Imperial Built in 1897 and extended in 1965, the Imperial Distillery boasts the largest pot stills in Scotland. Most of the single-malt is made for blending, but a small amount is bottled at an unspecified age.

BANFFSHIRE

Wedged between the counties of Aberdeenshire and Morayshire, the economy of this region is based on farming, fishing, and distilling. Ben Macdhui, the second highest mountain in the United Kingdom, and the Cairngorm mountain range are grouped along Banff's southwest border.

HAM AND HADDIE

Here is another of Alan Hill's exquisite creations from the kitchen of the Gleneagles Hotel, combining the warm, subtle flavor of smoked haddock with fine Ayrshire bacon and a rich Scotch whisky sauce flavored with the Cragganmore single-malt.

Serves 4

4 6-oz smoked haddocks (trimmed and boned)	1 sprig of thyme
salt and pepper	4 oz mixed peppers (cut in diamonds)
4 fresh sage leaves	2 fl. oz whisky sauce (see recipe below)
20 oz thinly sliced Ayrshire bacon	½ oz finely chopped chives
2 Tbs oil	
3 Tbs butter	

•Season the fish well, place one sage leaf on each of the fish, and wrap each with the bacon.

•In a saucepan, warm the oil and half the butter until foaming, and add the thyme. Then add the haddock and fry on both sides until just cooked.

•Saute the peppers in a little butter and season with salt and pepper, then drain and keep warm.

•Warm the whisky sauce and whip in the remaining butter.

•Place the peppers in the center of a plate and place the haddock on top. Pour the sauce around the fish, sprinkle with chives, and serve immediately.

WHISKY SAUCE

Makes one quart

1 fl oz olive oil	1 oz leeks
2 ½ lb crayfish bones (crushed)	4 oz fresh tomato, chopped
2 cloves garlic, crushed	2 oz tomato puree
1 sprig of thyme	7 fl oz dry white wine
1 sprig of rosemary	3 fl oz Cragganmore single-malt
1 oz carrots	
1 oz onion, chopped	1 quart fish stock
1 oz celery	3 fl oz veal jus lie

•In a large saucepan, heat the oil until smoking, add the butter, and heat till foaming subsides.

•Add the garlic, herbs, and vegetables, and cook until the vegetables are soft. Add the fresh tomato and cook until all the water is evaporated. Add the tomato puree and the crushed crayfish bones and cook five minutes.

•Add the wine and reduce by two-thirds. Add the whisky and reduce by two-thirds.

•Add the fish stock and veal jus lie. Bring to the boil, skin, and reduce by half. Strain through cheesecloth.

Aberlour

Ben Rinnes rises loftily above this distillery town, which takes its name from the River Lour, a stream flowing into the River Spey two miles (3.2km) southwest of the Rock of Craigellachie, a famous landmark in the history of the Highland clan Grant.

The town's name in Gaelic means "The Mouth of the Lour."

Aberlour-Glenlivet   Although there is a famous well here named after St. Drostan (or Dunstan), a sixth-century missionary said to have been a nephew of St. Columba, the first distillery is presumed to have been built in the 1820s, and was rebuilt in 1879 after a fire. Bottled at ten and twelve years, Aberlour has become one of the most popular single-malts in France.

Benrinnes   Ben Rinnes dominates the local landscape and rises to 2755 feet (839.7m) above sea level. The Benrinnes Distillery sits on its northern slopes at a height of seven hundred feet (213.4m), and water for both distilling and cooling comes from the adjoining Rowantree and Scurran Burns. Dating from the 1830s, the distillery was largely rebuilt and modernized in the 1950s. Benrinnes single-malt is bottled at fifteen years.

page 91: *An unusual bottle of Old Parr blended Scotch.* opposite: *The basic shape of the pot still has remained unaltered since Scotch whisky was first manufactured.* above: *The sealed entry to a still at the Macallan Distillery.*

Craigellachie   Built in 1890, this distillery overlooks the Rock of Craigellachie and the 1815 single-span iron Craigellachie Bridge, which spans the River Spey. Although much of its production goes toward blending, Craigellachie single malt is bottled at fourteen years.

The Macallan   The Macallan Distillery, at Craigellachie, was first licensed in 1824. This spot was a natural crossing place on the River Spey and a favorite with cattle drovers, who would stop off at the local farm for a dram or two. Standing within the distillery grounds is Easter Elches House, which dates from 1700 and has been extensively restored for use as a corporate headquarters.

Over the years quality, combined with a clever marketing strategy, has made The Macallan one of the world's most popular single-malts. Small stills are used and the spirit matured in sherry casks. Caramel is never used for coloring. The single-malt is bottled at twelve, eighteen, and twenty-five years.

Knockando

Around two hundred people inhabit the stone houses that, clustered together, make up this picturesque village alongside the River Spey, eight miles (12.9km) southwest of the Rock of Craigellachie. The community centers around the church, which stands beside the Knockando Burn.

Knockando   Built toward the end of the last century, then closed until 1904, this was the first distillery to introduce electric lighting. The distillery's name means "Black Hill" in Gaelic, and water is taken from the River Spey. The single-malt is bottled between thirteen and fifteen years, depending upon when the master distiller decides that the whisky is ready, and the brand labels denote the year and season of bottling.

Tamdhu   Established in 1897, this distillery sits under a hill on the banks of the River Spey. Renovated and modernized in 1948, the distillery's Gaelic name means "Little Black Hill." Tamdhu single-malt is bottled at eight, ten, and fifteen years.

Cardhu   Whisky was made illicitly at Cardow Farm for centuries before a distillery was licensed here in 1824. Its remote location in Upper Knockando, overlooking the River Spey, with

opposite: The Bowmore Distillery, which overlooks lovely Loch Indaal, is reputedly the oldest legal distillery on the Island of Islay. **above:** *An exterior view of the Dalwhinnie Distillery, which stands on the Drumochtar Pass on the road to Inverness.* **below right:** *The office and reception building at the Glengoyne Distillery in Dumbartonshire.*

water flowing off the nearby Mannoch Hill, made this the ideal spot to stay hidden from Excise officers. However, times changed, and with the opening of the Strathspey Railway in 1860, communications improved.

The Cumming family sold the distillery in 1893. It was extensively modernized in 1965, and features an attractive visitor center and a resident herd of Highland cattle. Cardhu single-malt is bottled at twelve years.

Dufftown

There is an old rhyme that says that while Rome was built on seven hills, Dufftown was built on seven stills, and certainly this town, situated on the River Fiddich, owes its existence to its distilleries, although only five remain operational. Dufftown was once the most notorious place for whisky smuggling; illegal distilling equipment was even hidden in the town's clock tower.

Dufftown-Glenlivet   Converted from a meal mill in 1896, the Dufftown-Glenlivet Distillery in the Dullan Valley uses the hyphenated Glenlivet affix. Although the distillery is close to both the Dullan and Fiddich Burns, water is taken from Jock's Well, which provides a seemingly endless supply. The single-malt is bottled at eight and ten years.

Glendullan   In 1902, just five years after the distillery was established, Glendullan single-malt was granted a Royal warrant by Kind Edward VII. Water is taken from the River Fiddich. An important component of Old Parr and President, a de luxe brand, the single-malt is bottled at twelve years.

Glenfiddich   William Grant, at one time a shoemaker's apprentice, built his first distillery in Dufftown in 1886. Employing his seven sons, he produced his first whisky on Christmas Eve of the following year. William Grant & Sons, now five generations old, is the largest family-owned distillery company in the industry, and ranks among the most successful Scotch whisky companies of all time. At Glenfiddich there is an impressive visitor center. Glenfiddich single-malt is bottled at eighteen, twenty-one, and thirty years.

above: *Scotland's distilleries are located in all kinds of landscape settings. However, many are hidden away, recalling the days when whisky smuggling was a way of life with the folk of the Highlands of Scotland.* **opposite:** *A bottle of Springbank single-malt from Campbeltown.*

The Balvenie Another distillery that remains in the hands of William Grant's descendants, Balvenie was built by Grant in 1892, close to his Glenfiddich Distillery and to the ruins of Balvenie Castle, a former home of the first Earl of Fife. Water for distilling is taken from the Robbie Dubh spring, and the Fiddich Burn supplies water for cooling. The Balvenie Distillery farms its own barley and maintains a cooperage (where wooden casks are made and repaired) and coppersmith's shop.

The Balvenie Founder's Reserve is bottled at ten years, Balvenie Doublewood at twelve years, and Balvenie Single Barrel at fifteen years.

Mortlach Mortlach in Gaelic means "a bowl-shaped valley." A distillery was licensed in this little glen outside of town in 1823. It subsequently operated as a brewery before turning full-time to distilling in the mid-nineteenth century. Process water is drawn from springs in the Conval Hills, with cooling water from the River Dullan. Mortlach single-malt is bottled at twelve years.

Ballindalloch

Situated twelve miles (19.3km) northeast of Grantown-on-Spey, this hamlet is home to three important distilleries.

Cragganmore John Smith, physically a giant of a man, had managed The Macallan, Glenlivet Wishaw, and Glenfarclas distilleries before building his own distillery close to Ballindalloch Station on the Strathspey Railway in 1870. He obtained his process water from springs on Craggan More Hill and pumped the cooling

DRINKING SCOTCH WHISKY

Over the course of many years, as Scotch has become an ever more widely popular drink, various rituals and taboos have come to be associated with its consumption. While these have served to increase the mystique and romance associated with Scotch whisky, they have also had the unfortunate effect of setting artificial limits on the many ways in which uisgebeatha may be enjoyed. What's worse, they have served to intimidate some drinkers from discovering the wonderful and varied world of malt whisky, out of fear that they might drink it the wrong way and be scorned for their ignorance by more sophisticated drinkers.

Some purists will insist that a single-malt is always better than a blend, and that it should always be drunk neat. But this is just as ridiculous as to say that red wine is always better than white, or that a hoppy amber ale, barely chilled, is always better than an ice-cold pale golden lager. The truth, of course, is that whether it's wine, beer, Scotch, or anything else, what's best depends on specific circumstances and on personal taste. So, while certain single-malts are indeed so silky to the palate that it is a shame to dilute them, the addition of a measure of water causes the flavor of many Scotch whiskies to bloom and to develop greater complexity. And while a rich, smoky, peaty single-malt taken neat is unbeatable on a winter's night in front of the fire, a hot summer's afternoon will probably call for a lighter blended Scotch, on the rocks with a liberal measure of soda and a wedge of lemon.

The point to remember is that Scotch is exceptionally adaptable, and its potential is being widened constantly. There is truly no wrong way to enjoy Scotch whisky.

water from the River Spey. Cragganmore single-malt is bottled at twelve years and features as one of United Distillers six Classic Malts.

Glenfarclas

Glenfarclas means "Glen of the Green Grassland," and legal distilling began here on the farm in 1836. In 1865, John Grant acquired the land and distillery, and they have remained within his family for five generations. The distillery's visitor center includes the Ship Room, which re-creates the first-class lounge of the SS Empress of Austria, a famous passenger liner. Glenfarclas single-malts are bottled at various ages from ten to thirty years.

The Glenlivet

In 1824, the fifth Duke of Gordon encouraged his tenant George Smith to apply for a license to build a distillery at Upper Drumin. Whisky had been made here illegally for several years, but so successful was the legalized venture that by 1858, a much larger distillery was built at Minmore, and under the expert guidance of Andrew Usher, a whisky agent, Glenlivet became heavily in demand overseas.

Glenlivet remains one of the best-known single-malt brand names in the world, and is bottled at twelve years.

Tomintoul

This is the highest village in Banffshire, situated at the foot of Carn Meadhonach on the River Avon, fourteen and a half miles

opposite: *The serving of Scotch whisky in a variety of bottles and decanters can be an art in itself.* **above:** *A long avenue of pot stills testifies to the large output of the Glenfiddich distillery.*

(23.3km) south of Ballindalloch. Whisky smugglers once frequented this area, and illicit stills operated unhindered for years.

Tomintoul-Glenlivet   A modern distillery was built in 1965 on a site five miles (8km) from Tomintoul, with water from the Ballantruan Spring. Although most of the spirit goes toward blending, a certain amount of single-malt is bottled at twelve years.

Advie

Located on the River Spey, eight miles (12.9km) east of the market town of Grantown-on-Spey, this small village is tucked into a rolling, picturesque landscape, dominated by the Tormore Distillery.

Tormore   Built in 1958, this was the first completely new distillery to be built in the Highlands in the twentieth century. The distinguished architect Sir Albert Richardson, a past president of the Royal Scottish Academy, designed the distillery, which is set against a thickly wooded hillside. Its white buildings, belfry, and houses for distillery workers make it a spectacular place. There is even an ornamental curling lake and a musical clock that plays "Highland Laddie" on the hour.

Water for the distillery comes from the Achvochkie Burn, which flows from Loch an Oir, translated as the "Loch of Gold." Single-malt is bottled at ten years, and at five years for export only. Although this single-malt is produced strictly in the Grampian Region, it is classified as Speyside.

Mulben

This tiny hamlet sits amid prime farmland five miles (8km) west of Keith.

Glentauchers   Founded in 1898 and rebuilt in 1965, then mothballed, Glentauchers is now back in production again, although most of the spirit produced goes for blending. Glentauchers single-malt can, however, occasionally be acquired through independent bottlers at different ages.

opposite and above: *Pot stills at the Dalmore Distillery, originally built in 1839. The distillery looks over the Cromartie Firth in the eastern Highlands.*

The Singleton of Auchroisk   A modern distillery dating from 1974, the name is derived from the Gaelic "Auchroisk," which means "the ford over the red stream." With eight stills, the water comes from Dorie's Well. The Auchroisk single-malt is bottled at ten years.

Keith

This small, agriculturally based town is surrounded by the River Isla and sweeping, open fields fringed with clusters of woodland.

Aultmore   The Gaelic "Allt Mhor" means "Big Burn," which is appropriate given that this distillery takes its water from a series of mountain springs that come together in one big burn on a nearby hillside. Peat is taken from a deposit at Foggie Moss.

The owner of the Benrinnes Distillery built a distillery here in 1895, but the present building dates from 1971. Aultmore single-malt is bottled at twelve years.

above: *A bottle of Royal Lochnagar sits invitingly on the bar at the Gleneagles Hotel.*   **opposite:** *Fields of barley sway in the wind before being harvested for malting.*

SMOKED PLATE WITH A LAGAVULIN VINAIGRETTE

One of the favorite dishes to be had at The Clifton House is a deceptively simple plate of smoked fish with J. Gordon McIntyre's own Lagavulin Vinaigrette. As he describes it, the plate includes "smoked salmon, smoked trout, and smoked halibut, all from Dave Stewart, our wonderful local smoker at Nairn. He also provides smoked prawns, mussels, chicken, and duck, decorated with mixed salad leaves, herbs, and Lagavulin vinaigrette."

LAGAVULIN VINAIGRETTE FOR SMOKED FISH

In a blender, combine the following:

1 cup white wine vinegar	2 Tbs honey
1 cup dry white wine	2 Tbs salt
juice of three lemons	2 tsp ground black pepper
3 small shallots, chopped	2 cup olive oil
1 small onion, chopped	½ cup walnut oil
6 cloves of garlic, crushed	½ cup grapeseed oil
	1 cup sunflower oil
½ cup of chopped fresh herbs (chives, tarragon, parsley)	1 cup Lagavulin single-malt

Put the mixture in a tightly sealed jar, and store in the refrigerator, where it will keep for months.

opposite: *The pavilion at Nairn, a popular holiday resort in Morayshire on the edge of whisky country.* above: *The picturesque Strathisla Distillery at Keith, in Banffshire.*

Glen Keith In 1957, Chivas Brothers razed the old Keith Flour Mill on the banks of the Isla River in order to build the Glen Keith Distillery. With peat gathered from Knockando and distilling water from the Newmill Spring, the single-malt was until recently largely used for blending. Glen Keith single-malt is bottled by the Seagram Company at various ages, usually ten years.

Strathisla Dominican monks ran a small brewery on this site beside the River Isla as long ago as the thirteenth century, and Fons Bullions, the holy well, which even today supplies the mash water, is said to be protected by water fairies.

Distilling began here in the eighteenth century and later, after being licensed, prospered as the Milton Distillery, changing its

name in 1950. Water for cooling is taken from the River Isla, and for distilling, from a reservoir filled from a spring in the nearby hills. The single-malt is bottled at twelve years.

Buckie

A picturesque little fishing town, Buckie is situated on the Moray Firth. Close by is Fochabers, a popular tourist resort on the east bank of the River Spey.

Inchgower This distillery was built in 1871 at Rathven, one mile (1.6km) from Buckie, and takes water from the Letter Burn and the springs at Aultmore. The Inchgower single-malt is bottled at fifteen years.

GRILLED FILLET OF ANGUS BEEF WITH CRANBERRY RELISH AND CELERY AND POTATO ROSTI, WITH A WHISKY AND WILD MUSHROOM SAUCE

Mark Barker is the Executive Chef at The Old Course Hotel at St. Andrews, a very famous golf resort and spa. After an afternoon on the links, many's the guest that's brought the day to a perfect close with this sumptuous dish.

Serves 4

> 4 8-oz beef fillet
> 1 lb cranberry relish (see recipe below)
> 4 celery and potato rostis (see recipe below)
> wild mushroom ragout (see recipe below)

•Season the fillets lightly with oil and grill until cooked to taste.

•Place 1 warm celery and potato rosti at top of each plate.

•Slice the sauteed beef fillet and place one in the center of each plate. Spoon relish over the sliced beef fillets. Then spoon ragout over top. Serve immediately.

RELISH

> 8 oz fennel, diced
> 8 oz celery, diced
> 1 lb. cranberries
> 2 oz coriander, chopped roughly
> 2 jalapeno chilis, split

• Saute fennel and celery in a little olive oil for several minutes, until wilted.

• Add cranberries, sugar, and chilis, and cook over medium heat for 25-30 minutes.

• Remove from heat. Find and remove the chilis, and add the coriander. Keep at room temperature until use.

ROSTI

> 1 lb celery, peeled and grated
> 1 lb potato, peeled and grated
> juice of 2 lemons
> salt, pepper, nutmeg

•In a large frying pan, heat a little olive oil. Add the celery, potato, lemon juice, seasonings, and saute for 10-15 minutes.

•Heat a little oil in another frying pan, and place a 4-inch round cookie-cutter in the center of the pan to use as a mold for the rostis. Place one quarter of the sauteed potatoes and celery in the mold, and cook over medium high heat.

•After one minute, when the rosti has set, remove the cutter and turn potato cake. Continue to cook until golden brown on both sides.

•Remove from pan and keep warm. Repeat procedure until you have 4 rostis.

WILD MUSHROOM RAGOUT

1 lb mixed wild mushrooms

4 Tbs unsalted butter

4 oz single-malt Scotch whisky

1/3 cup veal jus

1/3 cup double cream

4 oz green onions, chopped

4 oz tomato, peeled, seeded, and chopped

4 Tbs chopped herbs (parsley, thyme, sage)

•Heat butter in a saucepan. Add the mushrooms and saute until liquid thrown off by the mushrooms is cooked off.

•Add the whisky, veal jus, and double cream, and reduce by half.

•Add remaining ingredients, cook for 5 minutes, and remove from heat.

Banff

A market town and fishing port, Banff stands on the mouth of the River Deveron, sixty-four and a quarter miles (103.4km) north-west of Aberdeen. A bridge of seven arches connects Banff to the adjoining town of Macduff.

Macduff   The Macduff Distillery was built in 1962 and takes its cooling water, and the name of its single-malt, from the nearby River Deveron. The Glen Deveron single-malt is bottled at twelve years.

Kennethmount

A small hamlet, nine miles (14.5km) south of the town of Huntly in Strath Bogie, Kennethmount is near the rivers Bogie and Deveron.

Ardmore   Built in 1891 by the Teacher family, this distillery was extensively modernized in the 1950s although it still uses coal-fired stills. The single-malt is bottled at twelve and eighteen years.

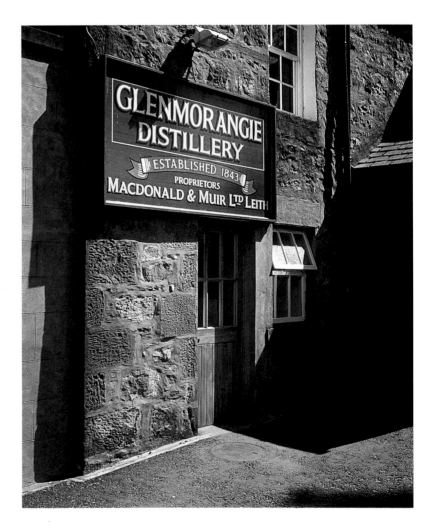

Knock

A small village, thirteen miles (20.9km) southwest of the towns of Macduff and Banff, Knock nestles into the slopes of Knock Hill.

An Cnock The Knockdhu Distillery was built on the River Isla in 1893 amid rich farmland from which there is a plentiful supply of barley and peat. The distillery closed in 1983 and then reopened under new ownership in 1989, when the brand name was changed from Knockdhu to An Cnoc to avoid confusion with Knockando. The An Cnock single-malts are bottled at twelve years.

SOUTHERN HIGHLANDS

The Highlands is a massive region, but Customs & Excise persist in using it as a single category of single-malt Scotch, encompassing every single-malt other than Speyside, Lowland, and Island.

The imaginary line that separates the Highlands of Scotland from the Lowlands follows the range of hills known as the Campsies and the Ochils, which stretch from above Glasgow east toward Perth and Strathearn, over-reaching the ancient town of Stirling, Scotland's historic "Gateway to the North."

For the purpose of categorizing single malt Scotch, the Southern Highlands begin in Dumbartonshire and encompass mainland Argyll, Stirlingshire, Perthshire, and Angus, reaching up to Dalwhinnie in Inverness-shire, and up the east coast into Grampian Region.

STIRLINGSHIRE

At the center of Scotland, this county is bordered to the north by Perthshire, to the northeast by Clackmannanshire, to the east by the Firth of Forth and West Lothian, to the south by Lanarkshire, and to the west by Dunbartonshire.

Dumgoyne

Southeast of the bonny, bonny banks of Loch Lomond, this pretty village in the Blane Valley sits on the slopes of the Campsie Fells, just north of the Highland Line.

Glengoyne Glengoyne Distillery, the name of which in Gaelic means "Wild Goose," dates from 1833. Taking its water from a fifty-foot-high (15.2m) waterfall tumbling out of the hills, it is the

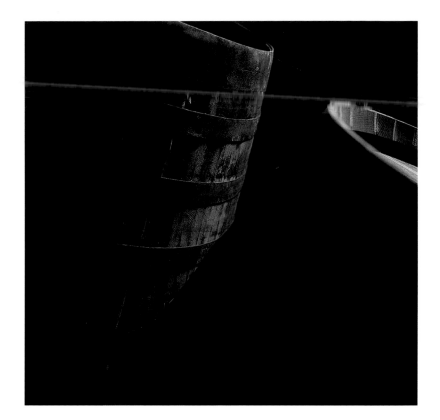

opposite: *White Horse casks sleeping at Lagavulin Distillery before being sent for blending.* **above:** *Casks are recycled after being imported from sherry manufacturers in continental Europe or bourbon manufacturers in the United States.*

only Scottish distillery not to use peat in its furnaces, and thus Glengoyne is the only one of Scotland's single-malts not to have even a trace of peat in its taste. It is bottled at ten, twelve, and seventeen years.

PERTHSHIRE

The ranges of the Ochils and the Sidlaw hills, parted by the estuary of the River Tay, define the southeast border of Perthshire, while the north and northwest districts are dominated by the Grampian mountains. The rich and beautiful valley of Strathmore, with glens and extensive deer forests, extends from the southwest to the northeast across the whole county. The fertile Carse of Gowrie stretches between the Sidlaw Hills and the Firth of Tay.

Doune

The ruins of an ancient castle, built in the fourteenth century by the Duke of Albany, Regent of Scotland, remain in this village beside the River Teith.

Deanston   The buildings of this cotton mill, built in 1785, were imaginatively converted to accommodate a distillery in 1960. Although the River Teith flows directly past, the distilling water is pumped from the Trossachs, the scenic and spectacular area of land that stretches from Loch Affray to Loch Katrine. Deanston single-malt is bottled at twelve, seventeen, and twenty-five years.

Crieff

During the sixteenth and seventeenth centuries, this pretty town on the banks of the River Earn served as a tryst, or market, for Highland cattle drovers, who came down from the north to meet buyers from the south. Today its easy access to spectacular surrounding scenery makes it a popular holiday retreat during the summer months.

Glenturret   Glenturret claims to be the oldest distillery in Scotland, and certainly it dates from the early eighteenth century, with some of the present buildings dating from 1775. Hidden as it is between two hills, the location must have been ideal for an illicit still and for smuggling. Glenturret's water supply is drawn from

above: *The Edradour Distillery was built in 1837 and is Scotland's smallest distillery.*   **opposite:** *Sunlight catches the copper of a still at the Glenturret Distillery.*

the Turret Burn, which rises high above the village in Benchonzie and Loch Turret, three thousand feet (914.4m) above sea level. The single-malt is bottled at twelve, fifteen, and twenty-one years.

Blackford

In close proximity to the famous Gleneagles Hotel, this small village is located on the slopes of the Ochil Hills.

Tullibardine   The distillery takes its name from a nearby wooded moor. The name is also associated with the great landowning dukes of Atholl, whose ancestral seat is at Blair Atholl to the north. Built in 1949, the distillery stands on what was a brewery in medieval times. Its capacity doubled in 1974 after a major renovation. The single-malt is bottled at ten years.

Aberfeldy

An attractive market town on the River Tay, close to the eastern end of Loch Tay, Aberfeldy lies just thirty miles (48.3km) from the city of Perth and its trading routes to the south. The railway line made this an ideal spot for the Dewars to build what would be the first distillery of a dynasty.

Aberfeldy   John and Tommy Dewar built this distillery in 1896 as a tribute to their father, who had begun life as a tenant farmer. The Pitlie Burn, which had supplied an earlier illicit still until 1867, provides the water. Near the distillery, the parent company has created a nature trail where a colony of red squirrels resides. Aberfeldy single-malt is bottled at fifteen years.

Pitlochry

A popular tourist town, Pitlochry is situated on the River Tummel, just off the main road north from Perth to Inverness. There are a number of excellent hotels and bed-and-breakfast establishments in the town, and an internally renowned theater, the Pitlochry Festival Theatre. Also in town is a hydroelectric dam with a fish ladder; the observation room enables visitors to watch the annual salmon run.

Blair Athol   The Blair Athol Distillery, which unlike the nearby town of Blair Atholl is spelled with one "l," dates from 1798, although it was licensed in 1826. Water is taken from the Kinnaird

above left: *The spirit safe at the Cardhu Distillery.* **above right:** *The spirit safe at the Glenlivet Distillery. The designs are basically the same, but always different in their details.* **opposite:** *A dram of Scotland's finest puts the perfect cap on a delicious meal at the Witchery restaurant, in Edinburgh.*

Burn and the mountain springs of Ben Vrackie, and in 1973 the number of stills was increased to four. There is an attractive visitor center and restaurant on the distillery grounds. The single-malt is bottled at twelve years.

Edradour   In the hills to the east of Pitlochry is the tiny, white-painted Edradour Distillery, looking almost like a toy-town. Said to have been started by a group of local farmers in 1825, the current cluster of buildings was modernized in 1982, and Edradour enjoys the reputation of being the smallest distillery in Scotland. The single-malt is bottled at ten years.

ANGUS

Bordered by Aberdeenshire and Kincardineshire to the north, and to the west by Perthshire, the county of Angus fronts the North Sea between Dundee and Lunan Bay. The countryside inland, through the wooded glens of Angus, becomes increasingly remote and scenic.

Brechin

A market town in the glens of Angus, Brechin once boasted a famous cathedral, now a church. It sits on the River South Esk, six and a half miles (10.5km) west of Montrose.

Glencadam   Licensed in 1825, this distillery was extensively modernized in 1959. It is located in a steep glen; water is taken from the nearby Moorfoot Loch. Although much of its production goes toward the blending of Stewart's Cream of the Barley, bottlings can sometimes be obtained.

INVERNESS-SHIRE

Bordered to the north by the inner Moray Firth, the Black Isle, and Ross and Cromarty, to the east by Nairnshire and Morayshire, and to the south by Perthshire and Argyllshire, Inverness-shire is the largest county in Scotland and stretches across the Scottish mainland to the Atlantic Ocean on the west. With Inverness as the Highland capital, the countryside, almost entirely made up of

mountains, lochs, and glens, is intersected northeast and southwest by the Caledonian Canal.

Dalwhinnie

In centuries past, Dalwhinnie was the crossroads for Highland cattle drovers travelling north to Inverness. Located sixteen miles (25.7km) south of the town of Kingussie, and three-quarters of a mile (1.2km) from the head of Loch Ericht, the landscape becomes increasingly dramatic heading west into the hills and glens below Loch Ness.

Dalwhinnie Standing on the Drumnadrochit Pass at a height of 1073 feet (327.1m) above sea level, this is Scotland's highest distillery location. Water comes in abundance from the mountains, flowing below ground for some distance before emerging as the Allt an t-Sluic Burn. Peat is extracted from the surrounding uncultivated land. Dalwhinnie single-malt is bottled at fifteen years.

Kingussie

At the heart of clan Macpherson country, Kingussie, located near the source of the River Spey, is the capital of the Highland Badenoch district. It is forty-six and a half miles (74.8km) from Inverness and twelve miles (19.3km) from the popular Aviemore ski resort.

Glentromie The Speyside Distillery was founded as a family business in 1990 at Drumguish, on the site of a nineteenth-century mill where the River Tromie meets the Spey. Glentromie single-malt is bottled at twelve years.

Tomatin

Nineteen miles (30.6km) southeast of Inverness, this small, remote village is located on the River Findhorn, which rises in the Monadhialiath Mountains and flows sixty-two miles (99.8km) northeast, through Strath Dearn to the Moray Firth.

Tomatin This distillery, although south of Inverness, is now included in the roll call of Speyside malts. Situated 1028 feet (313.3m) above sea level in the foothills of the Monadhialath Mountains, Tomatin takes its water from the Alt-na-Frithe Burn. With its twenty-three stills, it is the largest distillery in Scotland.

The main bulk of its production goes toward blending, but a certain amount of the single-malt is available bottled at ten years.

EASTERN HIGHLANDS

The Grampian mountains form the natural boundary between the Highlands and Lowlands on the east coast. The region encompasses Kincardineshire, Aberdeenshire, Banff, and Buchan.

KINCARDINESHIRE

Kincardineshire spreads out for 328 square miles (849.5sq km) along the coast below Aberdeenshire. Toward the north it slopes into the valley of the Dee, toward the south into the Howe of the Mearns, a part of the great valley of Strathmore.

Montrose

Sitting beside the Red Sea and at the mouth of the River South Esk, twenty-three miles (37km) northeast of Dundee, this sizeable historic town dates back to the twelfth century.

above: *The Lagavulin Distillery on Islay, where the White Horse blend originates.* **opposite:** *The Laphroaig Distillery, which supplies one of the components for the Long John, Black Bottle, Ballantine's, and Teacher's blends.*

above: *Casks sleeping at the Dalmore Distillery.*

Old Fettercairn   The original Fettercairn Distillery is believed
to have been located at the mouth of the River South Esk, where it
was hidden by the surrounding hills of Cairn O'Mount, part of the
Grampian mountain range. The present distillery lies nearby, in the
Howe O'Mearns, and at one time was owned by the family of the
nineteenth-century British prime minister, William Gladstone.
Since then it has passed through several owners and has been modernized. The single-malt is bottled at ten years.

ABERDEENSHIRE

The coastal city of Aberdeen is the focal point of this 1,971 square-
mile (5104.9sq km) area.

The coast is mostly bold and rocky, the surface inland hilly,
with moors and mountains to the southwest. The chief rivers are
the Dee, the Don, the Devon, and the Ythen. Granite is the principal rock, and the climate is less rainy than elsewhere in Scotland.

Old Meldrum

A small market town in the middle of Aberdeenshire, Old
Meldrum lies seventeen miles (27.4km) northwest of Aberdeen.

Glen Garioch   In operation as an illicit still toward the end of
the eighteenth century, the distillery was owned by various people
until 1937, when it was closed. In 1968, new owners, having sunk
a deep well to find a new water source, began production again in
earnest, taking peat from nearby Pitsligo Moss. The distillery is
very conservation-minded, and all excess heat produced is used for
growing fruit and vegetables. The single-malt is bottled at ten,
twelve, fifteen, and twenty years.

Ballater

This small town, close to the River Dee and forty-three and a
quarter miles (69.6km) southwest of Aberdeen, gained promi-

CHOCOLATE BREAD AND BUTTER PUDDING WITH A SCOTCH WHISKY SAUCE

A far cry from traditional bread pudding, this delicious dessert comes from Mark Barker, Executive Chef at the St. Andrews Old Course Hotel.

Serves 4

1 cup single cream

1 cup double cream

5 oz bittersweet chocolate, chopped into small bits

4 egg yolks

1 cup sugar

½ tsp vanilla extract

4 croissants (cut up)

•Bring the two creams to a boil together, add the chopped chocolate, and mix thoroughly.

•In a separate bowl, mix together the egg yolks, sugar, and vanilla.

•Add this mixture to the chocolate and cream mixture and combine thoroughly.

•Pour mix over croissants in a bowl and allow to soak overnight.

•Bake at 350 degrees Farhenheit using a bain-marie.

•Divide into four portions and serve on plates napped with whisky sauce and raspberry coulis.

WHISKY SAUCE

1 cup cream

¼ vanilla bean

4 egg yolks

½ cup sugar

4 tsp single malt Scotch whisky

•Heat cream and pour over the remaining ingredients. Return to the stove, and stir over very low heat for 5 minutes, not allowing the sauce to come to a boil. Remove from heat, discard vanilla bean, and serve warm.

nence thanks to its proximity to Balmoral Castle, which was purchased by Queen Victoria and her husband, Prince Albert, in 1952. With the royal family in residence each autumn, one or the other of the Scottish regiments is usually quartered in the town.

Royal Lochnagar   Named after the mountain that towers over the area, the first distillery here was built in 1826, but destroyed by a fire rumoured to have been started by rival illicit distillers. Today's distillery was built in 1845 and gained celebrity when visited by Queen Victoria and members of her family from nearby Balmoral Castle in 1848. Matured in sherry casks, the spirit is bottled at twelve years.

NORTHEAST HIGHLANDS

The Brahan Seer, a mysterious sixteenth-century figure, prophesied that when the coastline of northeast Scotland above Inverness was bridged, troubled times would follow. There are now bridges across the Moray Firth, Beauly Firth, Cromarty Firth, and Dornoch Firth, and as yet nothing too disastrous has occurred.

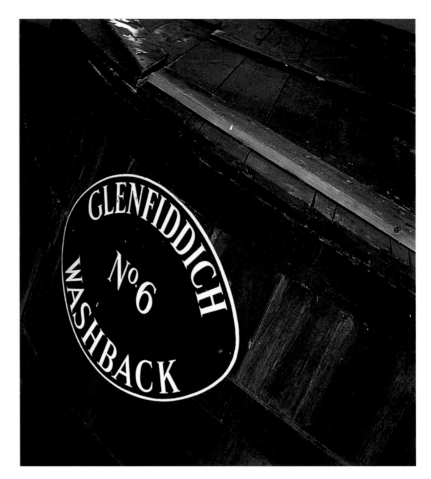

above: *Pipes and stills form the interior landscape of the distillery.*
above right: *Washbacks are normally made of pine or larch and house the wort, which froths and bubbles when yeast is added.*

Muir of Ord

Three miles (4.8km) north of Beauly, and thirteen miles (20.9km) northwest of Inverness, this hamlet lies in an area once notorious for illicit distilling, even late into the nineteenth century.

Glen Ord   There is evidence to suggest that the present distillery, licensed in 1838, was built on the site of an original illicit still with water originating from the Oran Burn, which flows from two lochs in Glen Oran, both one thousand feet (304.8m) above sea level. The peat, dug locally to fuel the furnace, has a strong heather mix, and undoubtedly this has contributed to the taste of the matured spirit. Glen Ord is bottled at twelve years old.

Alness

Situated on the River Alness, which flows from the Loch of Gildermory, close to Ben Wyvis, and southeast into the Cromarty Firth, this town benefited considerably from the North Sea oil boom of the 1980s. Overlooking the looming Black Isle to the south, Alness straddles the main road leading across to Scotland's eastern coastline and on to Wick in the far north.

above: *Wash is a weak, creamy brown form of alcohol from which the spirit which becomes whisky is distilled. Having flowed into the wash still, the wash is heated until it boils into vapor.*

The Dalmore   A distillery was built here in 1839, and twenty-one years later taken over by the local Mackenzie family. The spirit stills at Dalmore are noted for the curious flask-like chambers on the top. Situated against a wooded, hilly backdrop, the distillery draws its water from the River Alness. The single-malt is bottled at twenty-one years.

Teaninich   Captain Hugh Munro, a local landowner, founded Teaninich in 1817 as part of an operation to stamp out illicit distilling. So much local barley was being used up in the manufacture of uisgebeatha that the government was becoming concerned. After the Excise Act of 1823, the output of Teaninich Distillery increased by 40 percent. The distillery stands close to the River Averon, and in 1817 it was recorded as the only distillery north of Inverness to be lit by electricity. The spirit is bottled at ten years.

Tain

It is said locally that brewing and distilling have taken place here since the Middle Ages. The town of Tain, which takes its name from the Norse "thing," meaning "place of government," overlooks the

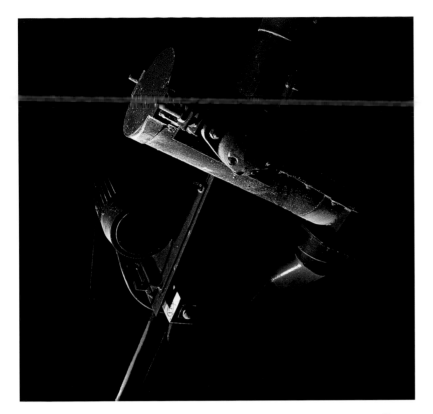

opposite: *The romantic gloom of the interior at the Glenturret Distillery.*
above: *The spirit pipe carries the raw alcohol to the reciever.*

Dornoch Firth, an estuary of the North Sea between Ross and Sutherland.

Balblair   The distillery at Edderton, on the south shore of the Dornoch Firth, five and a half miles (8.8km) northwest of Tain, dates from 1790, although the present building was erected in 1895. The surrounding areas is known as The Parish of the Peats. The single-malt is bottled at five and ten years.

Glenmorangie   Distilling in the area dates from around 1843, when a local farming family began it as a sideline. Glenmorangie means "The Glen of Great Tranquillity," which refers to the glen beside the Morangie Burn, formed in the hills of Tarlogie, and originating through layers of lime and sandstone in a forest to the north. The workforce at Glenmorangie Distillery is traditionally and collectively known as "The Sixteen Men of Tain," and the pot stills, which stand almost seventeen feet high (5.2m), are the tallest in the Highlands. The single-malt, bottled at ten and eighteen years, is available in sherry-wood, port-wood, and Madeira-wood finishes, and the whisky's flavor subtly reflects the influence of the casks used for maturation.

SUTHERLAND

Extensive deer forests and grazing land for sheep make up most of this area of inland mountain and moorland, bounded to the west and north by the Atlantic Ocean, to the east by Caithness and the Moray Firth, and to the south by the Dornoch Firth and Ross & Cromarty. The clans of Sutherland, most of whom originated from the Viking lands of Norway and Denmark across the North Sea, were known as the "South landers."

Brora

A small village at the mouth of the River Brora, seven miles (11.3km) from Golspie, Brora is dominated by the French chateau-style Dunrobin Castle, the ancestral seat of the earls and dukes of Sutherland.

Clynelish   The first Duke of Sutherland built this distillery in 1819 to provide a market for grain grown by crofters removed to the coast under the notorious Highland Clearances program, for which the Duke was held primarily responsible. The original distillery was called Brora and was eventually taken over, closed, then moved to another site. In 1968 a new distillery was built on an adjacent site and renamed Clynelish. The single-malt is bottled at fifteen years.

CAITHNESS

This large area of mountains, moors, and lochs in the northeast corner of mainland Scotland tops onto the Pentland Firth in sight of the Orkneys. A considerable portion of the land is given over to deer forests, but the coastline fishing industry is significant.

Wick

Located on Wick Water and Wick Bay on the far northeast coast, where the road swings west across the far right tip of Scotland, Old Wick consists of three parts—Wick, Louisburgh, and Pulteneytown—and is an important fishing center.

Pulteney   The Pulteney Distillery was built in 1826, close to the town of Wick, and produces a distinctive single-malt popular with the herring fishers of the neighborhood. As it is the only distillery in Caithness, there are ample supplies of water and peat available. Old Pulteney single-malt is bottled at ten years.

DALWHINNIE SCOTCH SOUFFLE

The Gleneagles Hotel is the only place where you can savor this exquisite dessert from the creative genius of Executive Chef Alan Hill.

Serves 4

SOUFFLE

4 spongecake bases

4 oz sugar

juice of half a lemon

2 egg yolks

1 oz Dalwhinnie single-malt

2 leaves gelatin (soaked)

1 cup double cream, whipped

MERINGUE

4 egg whites

8 oz sugar

lemon juice to taste

GARNISH

3 oz mango puree

2 oz raspberry coulis

½ oz plain yogurt

1 Tbs icing sugar

•Place one spongecake base into the bottom of each of four individual souffle molds.

•Combine two tablespoons of water, 4 oz sugar, and the lemon juice in a pan. Heat to 250 degrees Fahrenheit, then stop cooking and allow to cool for three minutes.

•Cream the egg yolks and slowly add to the syrup. Beat until cold.

•Warm the whisky and add the gelatin, letting it dissolve. Allow to cool and fold in the whipped cream.

•Fold the mixture of whisky, gelatin, and cream into the egg and syrup mixture. Pipe into the prepared molds, level, and freeze.

•To make the meringue, whisk the egg whites and sugar together until thick and stiff. Add the lemon juice, about one teaspoonful, and whisk for thirty seconds more.

•Remove the chilled mousses from their molds and place them with the sponge bases down onto plates. Pipe the meringue around the mousse, then glaze with a blow torch.

•Spoon three pools of mango sauce onto each plate. Pipe three spots of raspberry coulis between the pools of mango. Feather with the yogurt and dust with icing sugar.

above: *A swan steps gracefully across the seafront at Laphroaig Distillery on the Island of Islay.*

opposite: *A peek through the windows into the Laphroaig Still House.* above left: *Maintenance amd cleaning at Caol Ila Distillery on Islay.*

above right: *Alcohol and vapor are condensed into liquid in the pot still by passing through a worm, a spiral copper tube immersed in a vat of cold water.*

WESTERN HIGHLANDS

From Wester Ross in the far northeast to the Mull of Kintyre in Argyll, the coastline of the west, combed with countless inland rivers and lochs, and washed by the Gulf Stream, forms one of Europe's most beautiful wilderness areas.

Fort William

Under the shadow of Ben Nevis, this town was built to police the Highlands and was named after William of Orange, who became William III of Great Britain in 1689. It sits on the east side of Loch Linnhe sixty-five and a half (105.4km) miles southwest of Inverness.

Ben Nevis　This is one of the oldest distilleries in Scotland and for generations was run by the Macdonald family, descendants of "Long John" Macdonald, who claimed descent from the Lords of the Isles. The addition of a patent still enabled it to produce malt and

grain whisky under one roof. The single-malt is bottled at nineteen, twenty-five, and twenty-six years.

ARGYLLSHIRE

A scattered, maritime region, the mainland of Argyllshire is indented with far-reaching sea lochs. The peninsula of Kintyre extends about fifty-five miles (88.5km) south of the Crinan Canal to the Mull of Kintyre. Ardnamurchan Point is the most westerly projection on the mainland of Scotland. This is the ancient kingdom of Dalriada, colonized by the first Scots, who came from Ireland in the sixth century.

Oban

The gateway to the Islands, Oban was a tiny fishing village in the eighteenth century that grew into a major port and holiday resort in the nineteenth century. The hill above the town is dominated by a circle of columns, a replica of the coliseum in Rome, built by a

opposite: *The logo of the Oban Distillery on Scotland's west coast is instantly recognizable.* above: *A spirit tap at the Oban Distillery.*

above: *Evening falls on the northeastern coast of Scotland.*

local banker named McCaig, who ran out of money in 1859 before his project was completed. The aborted structure is consequently known as "McCaig's Folly."

Oban   The distillery is situated in the town, and was built as a brewery when the town was a village, around 1794. Water continues to be drawn from the peaty uplands of Ardconnel a mile (1.6km) away, and a visitor's center has been opened. One of United Distiller's Classic Malts, the spirit is bottled at fourteen years.

THE HEBRIDES

The islands off the west coast of Scotland are known collectively as The Hebrides. About one hundred of them are inhabited. Because of the changeable climate and exposure to the Atlantic winds, the land is unsuitable for corn crops. Cattle, sheep, weaving, and distilling have long been the staple industries.

THE ISLAND OF ISLAY AND ITS SEVEN DISTILLERIES

Islay, located off Kintyre on the west side of the Sound of Sleat, is the southernmost island of the Inner Hebrides. The coast is low, the interior mountainous. The large deposits of blue-black peat that are available inland give the single-malts of Islay their strongly identifiable character: peaty and salty, distinctly iodine.

Twelve miles (19.3km) southeast of Bowmore, this small village has a lighthouse that rises forty-eight feet (14.6m) above the high water mark.

Ardbeg   Established around 1815, the water is obtained from Loch Arinambeast and Loch Uigeadale. The distillery has opened and closed regularly in recent years, but the single-malt is available, bottled at ten years of age.

left: *Glenturret Distillery claims to be Scotland's oldest distillery. There certainly was an illicit still in operation in the neighbourhood as early as 1717.* **above:** *Even enormous copper pot stills grow old and have to be replaced from time to time.*

Lagavulin Once moonshiners manufactured and smuggled illicit whisky to the mainland on a nightly basis. The distillery, which stands beside a small bay, dates from around 1810, but the owners went into partnership with Peter Mackie, the great nineteenth-century whisky baron who founded the White Horse Company. Lagavulin in Gaelic means "The Mill of the Valley," and water is drawn from lochs in the hills of Solan. The single-malt is bottled at sixteen years.

above: *Distilleries are always located close to water. Some, however, have become part of the landcsape.* **opposite:** *The Glenturret Distillery, which stands close to the river Turret in Perthshire.*

LIQUEURS

Although single-malts are considered by many to be the ultimate after-dinner drink, it is hardly surprising that several whisky liqueurs have been created. The most famous of these, of course, is Drambuie, but the others each have their individual charms and always make for a pleasant after-dinner treat.

Drambuie

The legend goes that Bonny Prince Charlie, fleeing from his defeat at the Battle of Culloden in 1746, took refuge with the Mackinnon family on the island of Skye. In gratitude for their kindness, he presented them with the recipe for his favorite drink, Drambuie. The recipe, which remains a secret to outsiders, has been passed down through the generations and is always kept by the wife of the eldest Mackinnon son. The company is based in West Lothian.

Columba Cream

Based on a traditional recipe, this blend of five single-malts with cream and honey is produced on the isle of Mull by John Murray & Co., which is based at Calgary. They have a bottling and blending plant at Perth.

Glayva

In the Gaelic language, Glayva means "very good." This syrupy liqueur combines aged whisky, a syrup of herbs, aromatic oils, and honey. Glayva was first produced in Edinburgh by Ronald Morrison & Co., but sold on, passing to Whyte & Mackay.

Stag's Breath

Meikles of Scotland, a small family firm based at Newtonmore, on Speyside, began making this liqueur in 1989. The name is taken from the fictional blend made famous in Compton Mackenzie's hilarious novels about Highland life during the mid-twentieth century. Fermented honey and Speyside single-malt is used, and the bottle's label has a distinctive art deco label.

above: *The pagoda roof presents an interesting outline against the sky.*

Laphroaig   Originally an illicit distillery, Laphroaig appeared around 1820, and is one of the few to retain a hand-turned malt floor. Considered one of the outstanding single-malts from Islay, it is bottled at ten years and fifteen years.

Bowmore

This is Islay's capital, a "planned" village dating from 1768 and famous for its celebrated round church. Bowmore stands on a sea loch known locally as "Lovely Lochindaal."

Bowmore   Built in 1779, the Bowmore Distillery takes its water from the Laggan River and retains the tradition of turning the barley on the malting floor by hand. The barley is then dried in kilns heated by the local blue-black peat. The finished malt has a strong flavor, heavy and smoky. It is matured in either American oak bourbon casks or Spanish sherry casks. It is bottled at ten, twelve, seventeen, and twenty-one years.

Bruichladdich   Built in 1881 and located north of Bowmore, this is Scotland's most westerly distillery, and because its water is drawn from inland, the single-malt is not as heavy as the other Islay malts. Single-malts from Bruichladdich are bottled at ten, fifteen, and twenty-one years.

Port Askaig

A small port situated on a tiny bay on the northeast coast of the island, Port Askaig looks toward the island of Jura.

Bunnahabhain   Founded in 1881, the distillery looks like a chateau and is located where the River Margadale flows into the Sound of Islay. The pot stills are pear-shaped. Along with houses for the distillery workers, the owners built a school, a library, and villas for the excise men. Bunnahanhain single-malt is bottled at twelve years.

Caol Ila   Dating from 1846, Caol Ila overlooks the Sound of Islay from which it takes the Gaelic name. The distillery has been rebuilt twice, at a one hundred-year interval. From a private wharf, the distillery receives barley and ships the finished whisky to the mainland. Caol Ila single-malt is bottled at twelve years old.

ISLE OF ARRAN

An island in the Firth of Clyde, Arran is twenty miles (32.2km) long and eight to ten and a half miles wide (12.9km to 16.9km). The landscape in the north and northwest is mountainous, rising to Goatfell at 2865 feet (873.3m). Broddick Castle, the former home of the dukes of Hamilton and Montrose, is a major tourist attraction, managed by the National Trust for Scotland.

Isle of Arran   In 1993, Harold Currie, a former managing director of Chivas Regal, built a distillery close to the coastal village of Lochranza in the north of the island. Water is taken from a spring feeding Loch na Davie, one thousand feet (304.8m) above sea level, and bondholders who bought stakes in the project will receive the first cases of the bottled single-malt in 2001.

ISLE OF MULL

Separated from mainland Argyllshire by the Sound of Mull and the Firth of Lorne, seven miles (11.3km) west of Oban, Mull has a rugged coastline. There are several inland freshwater lochs, and the principal town is Tobermory.

above: *At the Bowmore Distillery on Islay, the exterior buildings appear to have been influenced by the art deco movement.*

Tobermory A distillery known as Ledaig was built in the early eighteenth century on the site of the present Tobermory distillery and has experienced mixed success. Happily it is now back in production. There is a visitor center and shop, and the wooded site overlooks the sea. The single-malt is bottled between seven and eight years.

ISLE OF SKYE

A bridge now spans the Sound of Sleat to Scotland's most romantic island, the largest in the Inner Hebrides. The island can also be reached by ferry from Mallaig to Armadale, and from Glen Elg to Kylrea. The Cuillin Hills dominate the landscape, and Portree is the major town. In ancient times Clan Donald and Clan Macleod were the most prominent families on the island. Their castles of Dunvegan and Armadale still survive.

Talisker Established in 1830, the distillery premises were eventually moved to the west side of the island on the shores of Loch Harport. Water for distilling is taken from the nearby Carbost Burn. Ownership has changed several times in its history, but it is

SCOTCH WHISKY AND THE COCKTAIL

While traditionalists will abhor the concept of a Scotch whisky cocktail, the idea of Scotch as a mixer is hardly a new thing. During the seventeenth and eighteenth centuries, it was common for whisky to be served as a punch at social gatherings, with sugar and fruit mixed in to dilute the strong taste. Today, young people, especially, add Coca-Cola, Irn Bru, or lemonade. There is nothing shocking about this. It is all a question of individual preference.

Blended Scotch is recommended for most cocktails. The following are just a few examples of what can be done.

EAGLES EYE COCKTAIL
From The Gleneagles Hotel

Combine equal measures of Scotch whisky and peach Schnapps with a dash of egg white, and pour over ½ glass of lemonade. Garnish with a slice of orange.

SCOTCH TOM COLLINS
From The Scotch Whisky Association

Pour a large measure of Scotch whisky over ice in a large glass, add five or six squirts of lemon juice, and top with club soda.

WHISPER

Combine equal measures of Scotch, French vermouth, and Italian vermouth. Serve over cracked ice.

SCOTCH WHISKY TODDY

Place a spoonful of sugar and lemon juice in a warm glass and add enough boiling water to dissolve the sugar. Add a generous measure of Scotch and stir with a silver spoon, pour in more boiling water, and top off with more Scotch. Stir well.

ATHOLL BROSE

Mix an equal quantity of honey (preferably heather honey) and fine oatmeal in a little cold water. Add Scotch and stir until frothy. Bottle and keep for two days before serving. Two pints of whisky will be needed for a half-pound of honey and a half-pound of oatmeal.

opposite: At the Gleneagles Hotel, a newly renovated Scotch bar offers guests an astonishing variety of single-malts. **above left:** *Magnus Herron is the head barman at the Gleneagles Hotel.* **above right:** *Regis Lemaître from France is the bar manager at the Old Course Hotel, St. Andrews.*

now under the United Distillers umbrella. Talisker single-malt is bottled at eight and ten years.

ISLE OF JURA

Separated from Islay by the Sound of Islay, and from Knapdale and Lorne on the mainland by the Sound of Jura, the island is famous for the great whirlpool of Corrievreckan. In the southern part of the island spring up three conical peaks, known as the Paps of Jura. The main town is Craighouse.

Isle of Jura   Illicit stills operated from the spot where the Isle of Jura Distillery was first built in 1810. It was revived in 1956 by two local landowners who, with support from the industry, began production in 1963. Later the distillery was acquired by the Whyte & Mackay Group. The single-malt is bottled at ten years.

ORKNEY

Located across the Pentland Firth at the top of Scotland is this chain of seventy islands, thirty of which are inhabited. The largest is known as Mainland, home to the major towns of Kirkwall and Stromness. For five hundred years, these islands were part of

Norway and Denmark. They passed to Scotland in 1469 as part of the dowry of Queen Margaret, the Danish bride of James III.

Highland Park   This distillery stands on a hill overlooking Kirkwall on the site of an eighteenth-century bothy that belonged to an illicit distiller named Magnus Eunson. He was a United Presbyterian church officer who avoided being caught by hiding his whisky-making equipment in the church pulpit.

The distillery has its own maltings and imports barley from the mainland. Two local wells supply the water. Orkney peat has a unique aroma, rich and heathery. The single-malt is bottled at twelve years.

Scapa   Built in 1885, the distillery has had several owners and is currently under the Allied Distillers umbrella. Overlooking Scapa Flow, where the German fleet was scuttled during World War I, the distillery falls just short of being the northernmost in Scotland. At present the distillery has suspended production, but there is some suggestion that Allied Distillers will start production again soon. The eight-year-old single-malt is rare, but available.

CONCLUSION

Scotch whisky has come a long way since the early Christian missionaries began to distill uisgebeatha in their monastries and distribute it around the Highlands of Scotland. Today its ditillation has developed into a world-wide industry, with the single-malts and blended whiskies produced in Scotland traveling to the far corners of the earth.

Scotch whisky is Scotland's largest net export earner, and it accounts for 80 percent by value of all exports of alcoholic drinks from the United Kingdom. Approximately 70 million cases of Scotch are distributed annually throughout the United Kingdom and international markets, and the demand is growing steadily as Asian, African, and Eastern European markets become aware of the pleasure of Scotch whisky.

Scotch whisky, be it single-malt or blended, is a social drink. The taste is clean and invigorating, and its character exudes sophistication. In times of celebration, it creates joy. It inspires courage and offers consolation to succeeding generations in times of stress, and there are even those in the medical profession who insist that, imbibed in moderation, Scotch whisky prolongs active life. Above all, the sharing of a dram symbolizes hospitality and friendship. For all these reasons and more, people who believe in sociability and living the good life, wherever they may be, will continue to drink Scotch for as long as the Scots continue to make it.

opposite: *The view from the boathouse at the Gleneagles Hotel, where guests may relax and enjoy the beauty of the Scottish countryside.*

BIBLIOGRAPHY

Barnard, Alfred. *The Whisky Distilleries of the United Kingdom*. New
     edition with an introduction by Ian Glen. London:Newton Abbot,
     1969 (originally published London, 1887).

Brander, Michael. *The Original Scotch*. London: Hutchison, 1984.

Brander, Michael. *The Original Guide to Scotch Whisky*. East Lothian: The
     Gleneil Press, 1995.

Cooper, Derek. *Guide to the Whiskies of Scotland*. London: Pitman, 1978.

Jackson, Michael. *The World Guide to Whisky*. London: Dorling
     Kindersley, 1987.

McMurphy, Brian. *The World Book of Whiskey*. Chicago: Rand McNally,
     1979.

Martine, Roddy. *Scotland: The Land and the Whisky*. Photography by
     Patrick Douglas-Hamilton. London: John Murray in association
     with The Keepers of the Quaich, 1994.

Daichess, David. *Scotch Whisky: Its Past and Present*. Rev. ed. London:
     Andrew Deutsch, 1978.

Skipworth, Mark. *The Scotch Whisky Book*. London: Hamlyn, 1987.

Slaughter, Thomas P. *The Whiskey Rebellion.*. New York: Oxford
     University Press, 1986)

*Whisky Galore: Songs, Stories, Talk and Secret Tips on the World's Noblest
Spirit*. Presented by Bill Torance with the Earl of Elgin and leading
experts. 2 cassette tapes. Edinburgh: Tel-a-Tale, 1996.

INDEX